The New Vegetarian South

The New Vegetarian South

105 Inspired Dishes for Everyone

Jennifer Brulé

PHOTOGRAPHS BY Fish.Eye Design

The University of North Carolina Press   CHAPEL HILL

Manufactured in the United States of America

Designed by Kimberly Bryant and set in Whitman by Rebecca Evans

The University of North Carolina Press has been a member of the

Green Press Initiative since 2003.

Cover photograph courtesy Fish.Eye Design

Library of Congress Cataloging-in-Publication Data

Names: Brulé, Jennifer, author.

Title: The new vegetarian South : 105 inspired dishes for everyone /
Jennifer Brulé ; photographs by Fish.Eye Design.

Description: Chapel Hill : The University of North Carolina Press,
[2018] | "Want to eat more plant-based meals but don't know where
to start? Love Southern-style cooking? This book will help. This is a
vegetarian cookbook for people who do or don't eat meat: for everyone.
And it is an especially neat book for flexitarians, those of us who eat
meat but want to consume less of it in favor of eating more plant-based
meals"—Introduction. | Includes index.

Identifiers: LCCN 2018008570| ISBN 9781469645162 (cloth : alk. paper) |
ISBN 9781469645179 (ebook)

Subjects: LCSH: Vegetarian cooking. | Cooking, American—Southern
style.

Classification: LCC TX837 .B877 2018 | DDC 641.5/636—dc23 LC record
available at https://lccn.loc.gov/2018008570

For my daughters,
Claire, Camille, Mimi, and Tess:
I am the luckiest woman in the world
to be your momma. May our travel
and food adventures never end.
You all are my best friends.

Contents

Acknowledgments   xi

Introduction   1
     Meat Substitutes Deliciously Demystified   5
     Making It Meaty: A Short Guide to Ingredients to
       Amp Up Meatiness   10

🌱 = vegan recipe

Appetizers and Snacks

🌱 Boiled Peanuts   14
🌱 Slow Cooker Boiled Peanuts   15
Warm Corn Dip   16
Kentucky Beer Cheese   17
Southern "Sausage" and Cheese Balls   19
Crunchy Buttermilk Fried Pickle Chips   21
Easy-Peasy Cheese Straws   22
Warm Sweet Onion Dip   23
🌱 Garden-Stuffed Summer Tomatoes   24
Sassy Pimento Cheese   25
🌱 Okra Chips   26
Deviled Eggs with Pickled Okra   27
Edisto Island Crispy, Curried Deviled Eggs   28
Pimento Cheese Deviled Eggs   29
🌱 Kale Chips   30

Soups, Stews, Broths, and Gravies

🌱 Corncob and Leek Broth   32
🌱 Roasted Vegetable Broth   33
🌱 Chickpea Broth   35
🌱 Senate Bean Soup   36
🌱 Umami Mushroom Broth   38

Corn Bisque		39
Georgia Peanut Soup		41
 Winter Tomato and Rice Soup		42
Tomato Essence Soup		43
Jambalaya		44
Gumbo		47
"Chicken" and Dumplings		49
Roasted Cauliflower Étouffée		50
Slow Cooker Green Tomato Chili		52
Brunswick Stew		53
Tomato Gravy		55
Sawmill Gravy		56
Herb Gravy		59
"Beef" Gravy for Rice		60
Chocolate Gravy		61

Hearty Main Dishes and Casseroles

Baked Nashville Hot Cauliflower	65
Nashville Hot Sauce	67
Southern Fried Tofu Nuggets	68
Charleston's Country Captain	71
Vegetable Purloo	72
Pulled "Pork" Barbecue	74
BBQ Sauce	76
"Crab" Cakes	77
"Oyster" Po' Boys	81
Carolina Veggie Burger	83
Slow Cooker BBQ Cabbage Rolls	84
Three-Cheese Broccoli Bake	86
Cheddar Corn Pudding	88
Tomato Pudding	89
Cheese Grits Casserole	90

p. 50

p. 81

p. 86

Savory Pies

All-Purpose Pie Dough   92
Ribbon Pie   93
Vegetable Stuffed Pie   97
Vidalia Onion and Clemson Blue Pie
    with Pecan Pretzel Crust   99
Roasted Vegetable Potpie with Cream Cheese
    Peppercorn Crust   100
Crunchy Tomato Pie   102

Vegetables and Side Dishes

Creamy Stovetop Mac and Cheese   106
Cheesy Garlic Bread Stuffed Potatoes   107
Salted Caramel Bourbon Pecan Sweet Potato Soufflé   109
Beans and Greens   111
Company Succotash   113
Old-School Buttermilk Mashed Potatoes   114
Crisp Broccoli and Smoked Almond Salad   116
Winter Creamed Corn   117
Individual Crunchy Mac and Cheese   118
Dirty Rice   119
Savannah Red Rice   120
Brown Rice with Mushrooms   121
Cauliflower "Rice" with Fresh Herbs   122
Hoppin' John   123
Baked Limpin' Susan   124
Roasted Butter Beans with Garlic   125
Slow Cooker Black-Eyed Peas   126
Chow-Chow   127
Cornbread, Sage, and "Sausage" Dressing   128
One-Pot Pimento Mac and Cheese   130
Fake-on Bacon   131
Fried Okra   133
Mississippi Comeback Sauce   134
Sweet and Tangy Coleslaw   135
Twice-Baked Not-So-Sweet Potatoes   136

🦃 Memphis Mustard Slaw   138
Rutmus   139
Wilmer's Potato Salad   140
🦃 Spicy Tomato Aspic   141
🦃 Potlikker Greens   142
Hushpuppies   143
Truffle and Mushroom Grits   144
Sweet Breakfast Grits   146
🦃 Overnight Apple Butter   148
Carolina Grits with Sweet Potato Swirl
   and Smoked Gouda   149
Fried Green Tomatoes   150
Pimento Aioli   151
Stuffed Yellow Summer Squash   152

p. 158

Pickles

🦃 Pickled Okra   155
🦃 Dill Pickled Beets   156
🦃 Easy Artichoke Relish   158
🦃 Tickled Pink Onions   161
🦃 Salted Carrot Coins   162

p. 161

Breads from the Oven, Skillet, and Slow Cooker

Cheddar and Herb Biscuits   164
Slow Cooker Pecan Cinnamon Rolls
   with Buttermilk–Cream Cheese Glaze   166
Easy Drop Biscuits   168
Hoecakes   169
Cornbread   170
Double Jalapeño Havarti Cornbread   171

p. 164

My four daughters inspired not only the writing of this book but the way our family eats, and even the opening of our family's restaurant, Davidson Ice House. These girls are strong-willed, smart, and sassy. Thank you, Bruladies, for demanding that we eat more plant-based meals. And thanks for making me laugh until I cry.

My editor, Elaine Maisner, was critical in developing the structure of this cookbook. Her experienced words and ideas were invaluable to the finished product.

Once again, my squad of dedicated recipe testers came through! Thanks to Aimee Symington, Hunter Busse, Heather Smith, Kim Kusterer, Anne Arms, Jane Stark, Gerry Mills, Ginny and Bill Ress, Betsy Morgan, Stacy Baker, Lisa Tzagournis, Leah Wagonbrenner, Jen Slosson, Heather Ward, and Julie Inalsingh.

My parents' influence runs throughout the pages of this book. Thank you, Mom and Dad, for sharing your love of food with me and for the tremendous support you've shown me.

Last, the gorgeous pictures in this cookbook were taken by Fish.Eye Design. Chef Natalie Lewis and photographer Annie Herrmann spent countless hours styling and photographing my recipes—I couldn't have found a more talented team!

Acknowledgments

The New Vegetarian South

Want to eat more plant-based meals but don't know where to start? Love southern-style cooking? This book will help. This is a vegetarian cookbook for people who do or don't eat meat: for everyone. And it is an especially neat book for flexitarians—those of us who eat meat but want to consume less of it in favor of eating more plant-based meals.

Over the past twenty-five years of writing about food, I've witnessed both here in the South, my longtime home, and all over the United States an increase in plant-based eating. It has gone from fad to trend to, today, a way of life for many families. But what is wonderful—and what I focus on in *The New Vegetarian South*—is that southern food traditions have always emphasized vegetarian dishes—they just didn't call it vegetarian. A tomato pie is a summertime treat, not a vegetarian dish. The same goes for fresh succotash or warm buttered biscuits.

Although all of the recipes in this book are vegetarian or vegan, this is not a health-food cookbook. Many of the recipes are healthier because of the absence of meat, but that's not the point. Some of the recipes in this book are classic southern recipes that go back generations, having always been meat-free, and I present my spin on them. In other recipes, I simply replace meat with plant-based ingredients while keeping the preparation, method, or seasoning (or all three) the same. In some cases, this results in healthier dishes, but in all cases, the most important factor, which outweighs all others, is that the end result be absolutely delectable.

Back in the day, meat was served sparingly in the South, mainly because it was costly but also because the southern growing season is long and home gardens are prolific. A ripe tomato and mayonnaise sandwich with a handful of crispy potato chips is the perfect summertime lunch—meat would be superfluous to this meal.

Just a few generations ago, many southerners would raise a precious hog to supply the family with meat for the year. You'd better believe they used every invaluable bit of the critter: smoked jowls or neck bones seasoned the potlikker for greens, knuckles were pickled and canned, chitterlings were fried, tails and ears were tossed in soups and gravies, and hams were salted and smoked. Fried chicken was a treat and usually served only on Sunday, after church. The rest of the week, southerners enjoyed steaming pots of pinto beans with cornbread and buttermilk or brown gravy over rice and pimento cheese sandwiches. Simple, beautiful, healthy meals that just happened not to have meat at the center of the plate.

As you can see, such flexitarian eating has a long-standing, beloved heritage in the South. This book celebrates that heritage in today's kitchen.

I'm not in fact a vegetarian, but I eat that way a lot. What started as occasionally and by chance eating vegetarian meals has blossomed into an intentional effort to eat more plant-based meals and fewer that contain meat.

Plant-based eating is, I believe, a sustainable way to live, one that is good for my family's health and for the health of the planet. Beyond that—and although I believe in the natural food chain—for me, the reason to eat less meat is mainly a humanitarian one, as I care greatly about animal welfare. The poultry, fish, and meat that is sold in most conventional grocery store chains differs from the more personally raised animals from small farms that were consumed by our forebears generations ago. Today, the vast majority of poultry and meat is, sadly, factory farmed. Increasing amounts of fish and shellfish are, too. Given my sense of responsibility, I try to put my money where my mouth is, and when I do prepare poultry, fish, and meat, I buy it from sources that ensure that the animals have been treated humanely and raised ethically.

I have friends who refer to themselves as *pescitarians*, because they eat vegetarian food plus seafood. Other friends may have no label but eat vegetarian food plus poultry and seafood. Still others eat primarily a plant-based diet but are occasionally drawn to indulge in a juicy burger. I call all of these friends, and myself, *flexitarians*. We usually eat meals that are vegetarian (without poultry, fish, or meat) or even vegan (no animal products at all, including milk, butter, cheese, and eggs), but we do sometimes eat meat. The main point is that we are reducing the amount of meat we consume by quite a bit: about 70 percent.

It has taken me—a classically trained chef, recipe writer, and cookbook author—a very long time to go from eating meat with almost every meal to eating it just a few times a week. The first memory I have of intentionally eating vegetarian is from when I was four years old. Walking into my family's kitchen, I was accosted by the smell of burning walnuts. I swatted the acrid air around me as if to bat away mosquitoes. My mother had just discovered a spiritual lifestyle that embraced vegetarianism: nutloaf was her entrée, literally and figuratively, into this new way of life. The dish was such a disaster that, four decades later, my brother, sisters, and I still give her grief about it. We soon went back to eating the way our midwestern forebears had for generations: nutloaf replaced by meatloaf and ham loaf, accompanied by sides of buttery mashed potatoes and iceberg lettuce salads topped with bacon bits.

When I was six, my parents enrolled me in a transcendental meditation course in order for me to receive a mantra, learn about the maharishi, and discover enlightenment. It was then that I decided on my own to become a vegetarian—but my little psyche didn't quite want to give up meat completely. I remember so clearly being in the TM house, waiting for my lesson to begin, and looking at pictures of groovy, long-haired adults, their legs crossed, index fingers delicately touching thumbs and creating crinkly circles, eyes closed, faces awash with serene smiles. My TM teacher told me that through meditation I could achieve anything: I just had to will it, and it would be. My very sincere response to him? "I'd like a McDonald's Quarter Pounder with Cheese to appear in my hand right now." I was completely serious and incredibly excited at the prospect of this actually happening.

It's been that struggle ever since, wanting to be fully committed to being vegetarian and being *really* close but then . . . a restaurant hires me to develop fried chicken recipes, or it's the fleeting softshell crab season, or a plate of Jamón Ibérico falls into my lap, and I'm like, "Why do animals have to taste so good?!"

And let's be clear about one thing: as much as I am pro–plant-based meals, I firmly believe that incorporating them into one's diet should *never* feel like a chore or anything less than satisfying. In this book, I will teach you about all sorts of vegetarian ingredients that draw on the flavor profile and texture of meat, and I will teach you about special cooking methods that amp up the umami, or savory qualities, of these wonderful ingredients.

Take fried oysters, for example. I love fried oysters in a po' boy sandwich, and I wanted to create a vegetarian sandwich that retained the same toothsome crunch and mineral flavor of fried oysters. Oyster mushrooms are aptly named not only because their meaty texture mimics bivalves and poultry alike but also because of their beautiful, oyster-gray color. Dipped in an egg wash, dredged in seasoned cornmeal, and fried—voilà, oyster mushrooms make a remarkably crunchy, tender sandwich that many people will think is made of real oysters.

This book wouldn't be complete without a recipe for barbecue. In the South, barbecue only ever refers to slowly roasted or smoked pork. In this book, though, I take jackfruit and turn it into something to sing about. Ubiquitous in Southeast Asia and easily found here in Asian grocery stores or from online purveyors, jackfruit is the bounty of a tree in the fig, mulberry, and breadfruit family. When shredded, it looks exactly like pulled pork, and prepared with the right spices, tangy sauce, and a quick roast in the oven, it tastes remarkably like pork barbecue.

To those not familiar with tofu, the soybean product that originated in China and Japan, a delicate and delicious flavor awaits when you know how to cook with it. In my recipes, the mild nature of tofu provides the perfect base for Southern Fried Buttermilk Tofu Nuggets. The crust is savory and crispy, while the interior is tender and firm—an unbeatable combination.

Gravies are a great example of how southern meals can be turned into vegetarian-wow with the right seasonings and cooking methods. Typically, bacon drippings are the start of classic tomato gravy that, when generously spooned over a freshly made biscuit, satiates equally for breakfast, lunch, or dinner. My *New Vegetarian South* Tomato Gravy, however, doesn't start with bacon drippings—instead, I use a few special ingredients to achieve that smoky flavor and silky mouth-feel. Another gravy, Sawmill Gravy, is one of my all-time favorite comfort foods, as well as an often-requested dinner for my four daughters. It's a creamy white gravy traditionally redolent of breakfast sausage. My version uses vegetarian breakfast sausage that lends a taste so similar to the traditional Sawmill Gravy that I doubt anyone could ever tell the difference.

This book also contains an abundance of recipes for amazing vegan dishes that use no dairy or eggs. My Roasted Cauliflower Étouffée is an example of how absolutely satisfying a vegan main dish can be—you don't need to think of it as eating vegan, just as dining deliciously. You'll have the same satisfaction in the vegan Gumbo and the many other vegan recipes that I'll show you how to make.

For some of us, committing all of a sudden to a completely vegetarian or vegan diet can feel overwhelming. Your perception of it may be extreme, all black and white, as if you're eating burgers, steaks, and pork chops with abandon or you're relegated to eating rabbit food. My own experience is simple: go slowly. Moving toward eating more plant-based meals is best done gradually, I suggest, and not in a strict manner.

Let's face it: despite the high profile of farm-to-table southern restaurants and terrific cookbooks promoting contemporary approaches to the region's foodways, it is very hard for southern cooking to overcome its fat-and-grease-heavy image. This book of southern-inspired dishes aims to help you discover and cook food that is not necessarily vegetarian or vegan—though it is—but rather food that is often lighter, definitely fun to cook for any occasion, and always simply delicious to eat.

Meat Substitutes Deliciously Demystified

If you've got a hankering for a porterhouse steak, pretty much nothing will quell that craving but a porterhouse steak. However, there are loads of dishes where meat, poultry, or fish can easily, and quite often unnoticeably, be swapped out for a nonmeat alternative. This makes it a snap to decrease the amount of meat in your diet, eating meat only when nothing else will do.

In many instances, I find that I'm craving not the meat itself but its flavor profile: the salty, smokiness of bacon or the crispy crunch of fried chicken, for instance. Flavors and textures like these can be replicated with plant-based ingredients. Think of these meat substitutes as a jumping-off point; with the right preparations and seasonings, they will easily satiate the carnivorous palate.

Tofu is exceptional for its transformational ability; treat it right and it can be silky soft or firm and chewy, with nearly any flavor you choose. Tempeh, though less commonly known in the States, is common in Indonesia. It has a toothsome texture similar to that of pork. Seitan, unlike tofu and tempeh, is made of wheat gluten rather than soy. Its texture can mimic virtually any meat. Texturized vegetable protein (TVP) is derived from soy and works beautifully in any recipe that calls for ground or finely chopped meat. Then there are vegetables and even fruits that have the texture and sometimes look of meat.

Below is a list of the foods that I have found to serve as tasty and nutritious substitutes for meat, poultry, and fish. You may also find other very good meat-substitute products in the freezer section at the grocery store. (I've noted within the recipes that follow which brands I prefer for taste and texture when such an ingredient is called for.)

Tofu (Soybeans)

Silken, soft, medium, firm, extra-firm, or super-firm, tofu is often misunderstood and underappreciated outside of East Asian kitchens. Although the freshest tofu has a mild, nutty flavor, you can think of tofu as a blank canvas, ready to be transformed with the use of certain preparation methods, marinades, seasonings, and sauces. Like a boneless, skinless chicken breast, it can go from bland to outstanding with the right touch.

Tofu takes on flavor beautifully. In some ways, unseasoned tofu is similar to very mild cheese, and the two products are made in a similar fashion. Both start with a milk: tofu uses soymilk, and cheese uses animal milk. A coagulant is added to thicken the milk, turning it into curds and whey. The curds are cut, strained out of the whey, and pressed to condense into a firm block. At this point, dairy cheese is usually salted and often aged, adding flavor, but basic tofu receives neither treatment and so needs particular attention to flavor when cooking.

Tofu can be flavored very highly in a variety of ways, and it usually is, in my book. First, you can marinate and bake tofu. Submerging pressed or frozen (then thawed) tofu in marinade and then baking it is a wonderful way to infuse tofu with flavor. Simply cover tofu halves or pieces with marinade and allow them to sit at room temperature for thirty minutes or in the refrigerator for up to several hours. Remove the tofu from the marinade, pat the pieces dry with paper towels, and bake them in a 400° oven for up to an hour (depending on the size of the tofu pieces).

Saucing is another way to flavor tofu beautifully. Tossing tofu in sauce right after it has been fried, baked, or sautéed will ensure that it is satisfyingly doused in flavor.

The texture of tofu can be changed in a variety of ways, bringing it from soft to more dense and chewy.

PRESSING

Pressing before cooking releases much of the tofu's water (which imparts its bland flavor). Once the water is removed, the tofu can absorb other flavors through marinating, seasoning, or saucing. Pressing also gives tofu a firmer texture (if you purchase the extra- or super-firm styles, the work has been done for you). Cut the tofu in half lengthwise, line a plate with two paper towels, lay the tofu halves on the paper towels, and cover with two more paper towels and another plate. Place books or a heavy pot on top of the plate to press down on the tofu and let it sit for fifteen minutes.

FREEZING

Freezing changes the texture of tofu dramatically, taking it from super smooth and soft to chewy and toothsome—meatier. Depending on which brand of tofu you buy, freezing will turn the tofu from white to yellow; this is normal. Remove the tofu from the water in the package and place it on a plate or tray. Freeze the block whole or cut it into slices for faster thawing later. Freeze overnight or for at least six hours. Thaw in the refrigerator, in the microwave (briefly), or at room temperature before cooking.

SUBMERGING IN BOILING WATER

This process firms up the tofu while leaving it still very malleable and able to take on flavor. Slice one extra- or super-firm block of tofu into pieces or cubes, depending on the recipe, and lay them in a baking dish or a heat-proof bowl. Bring four cups water and two teaspoons salt to a boil and pour it over the tofu, fully submerging the pieces. Soak for fifteen minutes, then remove the tofu pieces and blot them dry thoroughly with paper towels before cooking.

Tempeh (Fermented Soybeans)

Tempeh is made from soybeans that are lightly fermented and formed into a cake. It is high in protein and cholesterol-free, with a much firmer, grainer, and drier texture than tofu. It works well sliced thinly and stir-fried or sautéed and layered into deli sandwiches.

Seitan (Processed Wheat Gluten)

If you don't have any gluten issues, seitan is a fabulously meaty choice. The texture is very much like the interior of a chicken nugget. Seitan is available either plain or seasoned in most large grocery stores. It can replace meat in virtually any cooking method—grilling, roasting, sautéing, or braising—with little preparation.

Texturized Vegetable Protein (TVP)
(Defatted and Dehydrated Soy Product)

This shelf-stable, inexpensive meat substitute is higher in protein than steak and is easy to incorporate into recipes. It comes in granules, slices, chunks, and strips and can be reconstituted with boiling water or, better yet, broth. Use it to make tacos, chili, shepherd's pie—any dish in which you would normally use ground or chopped meat.

Mighty, Meaty Fruits, Vegetables, and Legumes

The vegetables, legumes, and even fruits described next are invaluable sources for making southern-style dishes that traditionally use meat. You may not be familiar with them yet, but I'll show you how to use them step by step, and you'll soon find that your South has expanded mightily.

JACKFRUIT

Throughout Southeast Asia, jackfruit is commonly eaten fresh. Young, green jackfruit canned in water or brine can be found in Asian markets in the United States. Avoid buying jackfruit canned in syrup, as its sugary sweet flavor is entirely different from green jackfruit packed in water or brine. Jackfruit's texture is surprisingly similar to chicken, pork, and even beef. I've fooled meat eaters with the Pulled "Pork" Barbecue recipe found in this book. Another favorite idea is using jackfruit to make the Philly "steak" and cheese sandwiches.

MUSHROOMS

Portobello and cremini mushrooms have an earthy, beefy texture and flavor, especially when prepared the same way as beef, as in grilling, but I am most strongly drawn to oyster mushrooms. They taste similar to chicken or seafood: just try my recipe for "Oyster" Po' Boys in this book.

LENTILS

Cooked lentils are a good stand-in for ground meat; seasoned properly, they can take the place of ground beef in tacos and burritos, meat(less)balls, fried patties, burgers, chilis, and stews. They are extremely economical and shelf-stable.

BLACK BEANS

Like lentils, black beans make amazing veggie burgers (check out the Carolina Veggie Burger in this book), as well as stews, soups, and dips.

CAULIFLOWER

New approaches to this well-known brassica deserve their own section. The trick to making cauliflower meaty is to roast it in a very hot oven, around 425°, until it caramelizes and even chars in a few spots. Cut a head of cauliflower into thick slices (steaks) and roast with a bit of oil, salt, and pepper until golden with dark brown flecks.

EGGPLANT

I think of eggplant as the tofu of the plant world—it takes on whichever flavors it is seasoned with. Breading and frying thick eggplant slices, then covering them in tomato sauce and mozzarella, and baking everything until melted and gooey—you will likely not miss the chicken in this Parmesan dish.

CHAYOTE SQUASH

Pale green and round(ish), chayote squash from Latin America is now found in many U.S. grocery stores. Remove the thin skin and one seed in the middle before cooking. It's got a semicrisp texture, similar to an apple, with a mild flavor that makes it a perfect carrier for other flavors. Deep-fried or oven-fried, then slathered in buffalo sauce, chayote is a great stand-in for chicken tenders. Sautéed, then simmered, it becomes the foundation for a wonderful curry.

Making It Meaty: A Short Guide to Ingredients to Amp Up Meatiness

Miso Paste

Made of fermented soybeans, miso paste, a traditional Japanese food, is what gives miso soup its savory flavor, but miso paste is also wonderful to have on hand for other uses and recipes. It adds a depth of flavor and pleasant saltiness and can be found in most grocery stores, virtually all health-food stores, and all Asian grocery stores. White miso, yellow miso, and blond miso are fermented for a short time and are mild flavored, while red miso is fermented longer and has a much bolder flavor.

Parmigiano-Reggiano Cheese and Rinds

True Parmigiano-Reggiano has been aged, creating an unbeatable flavor, with nutty, almost fruity notes. You can often find rinds in the fancy cheese section of good grocery stores—snap them up if you do! Sold for far less than the whole cheese, the rinds retain the deep flavor of the cheese itself. Rinds are great simmered in broths, homemade tomato sauces, soups, and stews. Just remove them before serving.

Soy Sauce

The Asian roots of soy sauce go back at least two thousand years, and its preparation involves no fewer than six steps, including soybean fermentation and brewing. Don't mistake that flavorless brown liquid that comes in clear packets with take-away Chinese food for soy sauce—true soy sauce has a complex, salty, and somewhat sweet flavor. Although there are hundreds of types of soy sauce (with different applications) from many countries, in the United States, Kikkoman is a high-quality brand found in virtually every grocery store.

Tomato Paste

Tomato *paste* has the capacity to enrich recipes, giving them meatier flavor profiles without adding an overwhelming tomato flavor. It also thickens and colors recipes. You can find it in either a can or a tube.

Smoked Paprika

Smoked paprika is invaluable when attempting to replicate meaty flavors. A little gives background depth; more gives a true smoky essence.

Liquid Smoke

Liquid smoke is a natural seasoning agent that, in the simplest terms, is literally smoke and water. Similar to smoked paprika, a little liquid smoke adds a smoky nuance, while more adds bold smoke notes.

Smoked Salts and Peppers

Delicately layering smoked salts, peppers, and spices creates interesting flavors more complex than a single smoky note.

Onion Powder, Garlic Powder

Using dehydrated onion or garlic powder adds flavor without sodium. Be sure to find the powdered or granulated onion and garlic, not onion and garlic salts—then you can control how much salt to add yourself.

Onion Juice

Use a microplane grater to juice an onion. What you'll get is a very fine, juicy onion pulp, which gives a wonderful background onion flavor to foods without adding chunks of onion. Jarred onion juice can be found in the store, but microplaning an onion yourself imparts a much fresher flavor, of course, than store-bought.

Appetizers and Snacks

We are a nation of snackers; we love little bites of bold-flavored foods. Southerners are known for their gatherings, and cocktail parties, church potlucks, and tailgates are all perfect platforms for small bites. Whether served with a cocktail, a cold beer, a cup of coffee, or a glass of sweet tea, these snacks will whet the appetite and keep the party going.

Boiled Peanuts 🥜

2 pounds raw or green
    peanuts, in the shell
1½ cups kosher or sea salt,
    divided

Boiled peanuts are found in many parts of the South at roadside stands, country stores, and gas stations. I never liked peanuts much until our family moved to Augusta, Georgia, and I tasted the boiled variety. I had only ever known crunchy, dry roasted peanuts and for some reason didn't care for them. But the first time I tasted boiled peanuts, I was hooked! Boiled peanuts are raw peanuts (shell on and unroasted) that have been boiled in salt water for hours, until soft, velvety, and wet in texture and earthy and salty in flavor. Boiling peanuts highlights what they are—legumes (such as beans, peas, soybeans, and lentils)—vegetables that are usually cooked in liquid and served soft. One caution: if you are careful about your salt intake, it's best to skip this recipe—reducing the salt produces an inferior boiled peanut.

MAKES 8 SERVINGS

Place the peanuts and 1 cup of the salt into a very large pot (a pasta pot works great for this) and add water to cover the peanuts by at least 2 inches. Cover and set over high heat. Bring to a boil, stir, reduce the heat to medium or medium-high, and cover again with the lid cracked.

Boil the peanuts for 3 hours, then pull a peanut out, let it cool, and crack open the shell. It will probably not be soft or salty enough at this point (unless you were lucky enough to get "green" peanuts—peanuts refrigerated as soon as they were harvested—which cook more rapidly). If they're not salty enough, add the remaining salt. Keep boiling the peanuts until they are as soft as you like, usually 5 or more hours; replenish the water as needed. Serve warm. Refrigerate any leftovers in their cooking liquid. Keep refrigerated for up to three days, and eat cold or warm them before eating.

Slow Cooker Boiled Peanuts 🥜

Making boiled peanuts in the slow cooker takes a while, but it's totally hands-off and it doesn't heat up the kitchen, something every southerner appreciates in the summertime. This version calls for less salt than Boiled Peanuts because the goobers sit in the water for hours longer, absorbing all that salty goodness.

MAKES 8 SERVINGS

Pile the peanuts into a large slow cooker, pour in the salt, and add hot water to cover the peanuts by 3 inches. Cover and set on high. Cook for 5 hours, then check to see if peanuts are soft; if not, cook for 2 hours longer.

This can also be done overnight; just lower the heat to the warm setting in the morning—the peanuts will be fine sitting in their warm saltwater bath all day. Keep refrigerated for up to three days, and eat cold or warm them before eating.

2 pounds raw or green
　peanuts
¾ cup kosher salt flakes
　(such as Morton's)

Warm Corn Dip

3 tablespoons unsalted
  butter, divided

3 cups fresh or frozen
  corn kernels

¾ cup diced red bell pepper

1 small yellow onion,
  chopped

3 plump garlic cloves,
  microplaned or minced

8 ounces (1 block)
  cream cheese, cubed

½ cup sour cream

½ cup mayonnaise

½ cup grated Parmesan
  cheese

1 teaspoon Old Bay
  Seasoning, more to taste

3 green onions, chopped

Why is it that at every party or potluck, the warm, gooey dips are the first things to disappear? This recipe has sweet corn, vibrant red bell peppers, and the zip of Old Bay Seasoning. Old Bay became a mainstay in my spice cupboard when I was attending culinary school in Baltimore, Maryland, in the 1990s. It was developed to spice steamed blue crabs, but there are lots of other uses for it: toss potatoes with Old Bay and oil before roasting or add a few teaspoons of Old Bay into stuffing before baking—it adds a zesty zing to many dishes.

MAKES ABOUT 2 CUPS

Preheat the oven to 375°.

Grease a 2-quart baking dish with 1 tablespoon of the butter and set aside.

Sauté the corn, bell peppers, onions, and garlic in the remaining butter in a 10-inch cast-iron skillet or heavy sauté pan set over medium-high heat. Cook, stirring often until vegetables are just soft, about 5–10 minutes. Turn the heat off and stir the cream cheese into the vegetables to melt it.

Scoop the vegetable and cream cheese mixture into a large mixing bowl and stir until the ingredients are at room temperature. Incorporate the sour cream and mayonnaise, then stir in the Parmesan, Old Bay, and green onions. Taste the mixture: Does it need more Old Bay or a dash of salt? Gently spoon the dip into the prepared baking dish and bake for 30–45 minutes, until it is bubbly and hot. Serve with toasted bread, crackers, or raw vegetables (celery sticks are especially yummy).

Kentucky Beer Cheese

My great-grandfather was from Swansea, Wales. Wales is that tiny, bucolic country on the western border of England. I cherish the stories that my mother and grandmother have told me about my great-grandfather. An ordained minister, he lived with my mother's family in the United States when he retired from preaching in Wales. I heard about his gentle nature and that he sat in a small chair my grandmother embroidered for him to read his Bible every morning (I have that chair in my living room today).

I also heard stories about the foods he ate—most of them landing somewhere between bland and dreadful. The exception was Welsh Rarebit: sharp cheddar or Welsh cheese and beer that is melted together and spooned over toast. Leftovers firm up nicely in the fridge, creating a wonderful cheese spread.

When we lived in northwest England, we were just an hour from the Welsh border and vacationed there often. Eating the foods that comforted my great-grandfather in his country was a way for me to connect with him—to reach through time and experience exactly what he experienced, if only for a moment. I love that food can do that: transport us through time, from one place to another, through flavor and texture.

Kentucky Beer Cheese has all the wonderful flavors of Welsh Rarebit but requires significantly less effort: it takes less than five minutes to make and involves no cooking. Make it a day or two before you want to serve it, giving the flavors time to meld together.

MAKES ABOUT 2 CUPS

¾ cup pilsner beer, flat and
    at room temperature
2 plump garlic cloves
2 (7-ounce) blocks sharp
    cheddar cheese,
    cut into 1-inch cubes
1 teaspoon Dijon mustard
⅛ teaspoon cayenne pepper

If the beer isn't flat and at room temperature, pour it into a microwave-safe mug and zap for 30 seconds.

Place the garlic and cheese cubes in the bowl of a food processor and pulse until chopped small, about 20–30 seconds. Add the mustard to the cheese and start the processor. Then, with the motor running, add the beer through the feed tube, followed by the cayenne; process for about 2 minutes, until the mixture is smooth and almost fluffy.

Spoon into ceramic soufflé cups, a jar, or Tupperware and keep refrigerated for up to a week. Serve as a spread with crackers or pretzels or use as sandwich filler.

Southern "Sausage" and Cheese Balls

Classic southern sausage balls are an addictive party food. They taste like a sausage biscuit (heavy on the sausage) with sharp, melted cheddar—it is impossible to eat just one. But precisely because of all that sausage, they tend to settle like a weight in one's stomach.

Using vegetarian sausage "meat" solves that issue. I find that most vegetarian breakfast sausages are absolutely interchangeable with pork sausage—flavor, texture, and all—making these vegetarian sausage balls a welcome addition to any party buffet.

MAKES 25-30

Preheat the oven to 375°.

Spray a rimmed baking tray with nonstick spray.

If the sausage is in patties and frozen, thaw and then crumble it. If it's more the consistency of raw sausage meat, cook according to package directions and crumble.

Stir together the flour, baking powder, and salt. Add the sausage and cheese and combine with your hands.

Whisk the melted butter and eggs together in a bowl, then pour into the flour and sausage mixture and combine with your hands. Roll 25–30 walnut-size balls and arrange them on the greased baking tray.

Bake for 15–20 minutes, until golden. Serve immediately.

8 ounces uncooked vegetarian breakfast sausage (such as Morning Star Farms, Quorn, or Gimme Lean)

1 cup all-purpose flour

1½ teaspoon baking powder

½ teaspoon kosher or sea salt

8 ounces sharp cheddar cheese, shredded

3 tablespoons unsalted butter, melted

2 large eggs

Crunchy Buttermilk Fried Pickle Chips

These crispy little chips are dangerously good! Serve them with a side of Mississippi Comeback Sauce or ranch dip—crunchy and creamy. Take the extra few minutes to slice whole pickles into rounds; it's worth the effort.

MAKES 6 SERVINGS

Slice the pickles into ¼-inch rounds. You will get 8–12 rounds per pickle, depending on the size of the whole pickle. Place the rounds on a plate lined with paper towels, then place another paper towel on top and gently press to extract brine. This will make them crispier when fried.

Pour 2 inches of oil into a 10-inch cast-iron or other heavy skillet. Set, with the lid covered, over medium heat.

Whisk the buttermilk and the egg together in a bowl and set aside.

Stir the cornstarch, onion powder, garlic powder, seasoned salt, and cayenne together in a separate bowl and set aside.

Pour the panko into a third bowl.

Once the oil is hot and ready (flick in a drop of water—if it crackles, it's ready), toss 6–8 pickle rounds in the seasoned cornstarch, then transfer to the buttermilk and egg mixture, turn to coat both sides, then finally coat in panko, gently pressing the rounds. Lay the breaded rounds into the hot oil and fry about 2 minutes per side—just until golden on each side (turning them only once will keep them crispy, not greasy). Drain the fried pickle chips on a wire rack or paper towels as you continue breading and frying the remaining rounds. Serve immediately.

4 large, whole dill pickles (Klaussen is wonderful for this)

2 cups peanut or canola oil, for frying

1 cup buttermilk

1 large egg

¾ cup cornstarch

1 teaspoon onion powder (not onion salt)

½ teaspoon garlic powder (not garlic salt)

½ teaspoon seasoned salt (such as Lawry's)

Dash of cayenne pepper

1 cup panko

Easy-Peasy Cheese Straws

1 (8-ounce) block chilled
extra-sharp cheddar
cheese, cut into 1-inch
cubes

8 tablespoons (1 stick)
cold unsalted butter,
cut into small pieces

1 cup all-purpose flour,
plus more for rolling

½ teaspoon kosher or
sea salt

⅛ teaspoon cayenne pepper
(or more for a spicy kick)

2 tablespoons whole milk

Cheese straws are ubiquitous at southern cocktail parties. Salty, crunchy, and flaky, they go along perfectly with a drink. They are essentially a savory shortbread, as they are made of flour, butter, and cheese and can be whipped up from start to finish in 30 minutes: What's not to love?

MAKES ABOUT 50

Preheat the oven to 400°.

Pile the cheese cubes into a food processor and pulse until finely chopped. Add everything else except the milk and pulse until the mixture looks like crumbs, then, with the motor running, drizzle the milk in through the feed tube. The crumbs will come together to form dough.

Lightly flour a clean kitchen counter. Quickly form the dough into a ball and flatten it; don't overwork the dough. Place the dough on the counter and sprinkle the top lightly with flour. Roll into a ¼-inch-thick square or rectangle. Use a pizza cutter to trim raggedy sides (save and reroll the trimmed dough), then slice the dough into strips about 5 inches long and ½ inch wide (any longer risks breaking the straws).

Lay the cheese strips on an ungreased rimmed baking sheet (you may need 2) and bake, uncovered, for 10–15 minutes, until golden and crispy around the edges. Remove from the oven and either cool in the pan or transfer to a cooling rack with a spatula. Once fully cooled the cheese straws can be stored in an airtight container for up to 5 days, but they are really best the day they are made.

Warm Sweet Onion Dip

You don't need to use sweet onions, such as Vidalias, for this dip. Although they're wonderful, even potent red onions sweeten up after being caramelized. This is a dreamy dip, missing the sodium overload that comes with onion dip made from a dried soup packet; it's a bit more genteel.

MAKES ABOUT 2 CUPS

Preheat the oven to 375°.

Pour the oil into the bottom of a cast-iron skillet or heavy sauté pan and set over medium heat. Once the oil is shimmering, add the onions and cook, uncovered, stirring every 2 minutes, for 15–20 minutes, until the onions are very soft and beginning to caramelize (turn brown in areas). Pour in the wine, bring to a bubble, scraping up any fond (brown bits) on the bottom of the pan, and cook for 1–2 minutes.

Spray a 1-quart baking dish with nonstick cooking spray and set aside. Place the cream cheese, mayonnaise, Parmesan, and black pepper into a large bowl and mix until well combined. Add the hot cooked onions and stir well. Pour into the prepared baking dish and place in the hot oven. Bake, uncovered, for 30 minutes, until golden and bubbly. Serve at once with garlic toasts or crackers.

1 tablespoon olive oil

2 large yellow onions, finely chopped (about 4 cups)

¼ cup dry white wine

8 ounces (1 block) cream cheese, room temperature or softened in the microwave

½ cup mayonnaise

1 cup grated Parmesan cheese

½ teaspoon freshly ground black pepper

Garden-Stuffed Summer Tomatoes 🌱

2 pounds Campari tomatoes
(about 20 small
tomatoes)

3 tablespoons extra-virgin
olive oil

1 plump garlic clove, minced
or pressed

1 small zucchini, shredded
(1 cup)

½ small eggplant, shredded
(1 cup)

1 ear fresh corn, kernels
removed

½ teaspoon kosher or
sea salt

¼ heaping teaspoon
ground cumin

4–5 green onions, chopped

These ruby-red cherubs taste like a southern summer garden. Most baked tomato recipes call for rice or breadcrumbs and often meat. I wanted this recipe to let the vegetables shine and therefore left the carbs (and the meat) out. The cumin delicately accentuates the vegetables' sweet and savory flavors, adding a wonderful earthy background note.

I serve these warm from the oven with thick slices of crusty bread, but they are just as good served at room temperature.

MAKES 4–6 SERVINGS

Preheat the oven to 375°.

Use a small, serrated knife to cut into the tomatoes at an angle, removing the top. Scoop out the tomato flesh and seeds and place into a bowl. Press the tomato flesh through a wire sieve or fine strainer, capturing the juice that's pushed through—you should end up with about a cup of juice. Don't worry if some seeds get mixed in.

Place a 10-inch cast-iron or other heavy skillet over medium-high heat and pour in the oil. Add the garlic and sauté until soft and fragrant but not colored, then toss in the zucchini, eggplant, and corn. Season with salt and cumin and sauté for about 5 minutes, then pour in ½ cup of the tomato juice and simmer for 5 minutes longer, until the juice has almost evaporated. Stir in the green onions, then set the mixture aside to cool slightly.

Once the vegetable mixture has cooled slightly, lightly salt the hollowed-out tomatoes and spoon vegetable filling into each. Set the filled tomatoes into a 9 × 11-inch casserole dish that has been sprayed with nonstick cooking spray. Bake, uncovered, for 15–20 minutes.

Sassy Pimento Cheese

Sassy because this pimento cheese is colorful and has a little bite from the fresh jalapeños. Using all sharp cheddar (rather than traditional mild cheddar) amps up the flavor as well. This makes a great sandwich spread and is also wonderful with crackers.

MAKES ABOUT 4 CUPS

Mix together the mayonnaise, roasted peppers and juice, jalapeños, and onions. Add the cheese and mix well to combine. Serve immediately or cover and store in the refrigerator for up to 3 days.

¾ cup mayonnaise (such as Duke's)

½ cup chopped jarred roasted red peppers plus 2 tablespoons juice

1 fresh jalapeño pepper, seeds and membrane trimmed out, the rest minced

2 teaspoons finely grated yellow onion (use a microplane, if possible)

1 pound sharp cheddar cheese, shredded (4 cups)

Okra Chips 🟢

1½ pounds fresh okra

3 tablespoons vegetable or
light olive oil

1 tablespoon curry powder

¼ teaspoon kosher or
sea salt

Okra can turn from moist pod to crisp chip in about 30 minutes. This healthy recipe calls for minimal oil and a quick roast in the oven. Curry powder is a natural seasoning for okra, but use whichever seasoning powder you like.

MAKES 2–3 CUPS

Preheat the oven to 350°.

Spray 2 rimmed baking trays with nonstick cooking spray and set aside (or use just 1 pan and make chips in 2 batches).

Trim the tops off the okra pods and discard. Slice pods on the bias into ¼–½-inch ovals. Place the sliced okra into a large bowl and drizzle the oil over, then sprinkle in the curry powder. Toss with tongs or clean hands and pile onto the prepared pans; season with the salt.

Roast until the slices start to shrivel and dry out, 20–30 minutes, remove from the oven, stir, and flip over. Return to the oven for about 10–15 minutes longer, until crunchy. These chips are best eaten the day they are made; otherwise, cool and store in an airtight container for up to 3 days.

Deviled Eggs with Pickled Okra

I can't make enough of these when I bring them to a party or family gathering—they fly off the plate! Pickled okra lends a pleasing sweet and sour crunch to the soft, creamy filling—a little slice of pickled okra on top lets people know what's inside the deviled egg.

MAKES 24

Trim the tops off the pickled okra pods and discard. Mince 3 okra pods and slice the remaining 2 into rounds (to top the deviled eggs).

Pop the yolks out of each hard-boiled egg half and place them into a bowl. Mash the yolks with the back of a fork, then stir in the mayonnaise, mustard, salt, minced okra, and dill pickles.

Fill each egg white half with the pickled okra yolks and garnish with a pickled okra slice.

5 small pickled okra, homemade or store-bought

12 hard-boiled eggs, peeled and halved

3 tablespoons mayonnaise

2 teaspoons yellow mustard

½ teaspoon kosher or sea salt

1 tablespoon minced dill pickle

Edisto Island Crispy, Curried Deviled Eggs

6 hard-boiled eggs

1½ tablespoons
   mayonnaise

½ teaspoon Dijon mustard

¼ teaspoon kosher or
   sea salt

¼ teaspoon curry powder

Cayenne pepper, to taste

½ cup kale chips, broken
   but not crushed

Edisto is a barrier island off the coast of South Carolina that is affectionately known by locals as "Edi-slow"—the island pace is considerably relaxed.

Our family made Edisto our home base "Stateside" when we lived abroad from 2003 to 2010, and we savored every minute on that sunny island. For some reason, our family eats a lot of deviled eggs in the summer. There's something special about a creamy, hard-cooked egg straight from the fridge.

MAKES 12

Pop the yolks out of each hard-boiled egg half and place them into a bowl. Mash the yolks with the back of a fork, then stir in the mayonnaise, mustard, salt, curry powder, and 1–2 dashes cayenne.

Fill egg whites with the yolk mixture and, if desired, sprinkle a tiny amount of cayenne on top. Just before serving, arrange shards of kale chips atop the filled eggs.

Pimento Cheese Deviled Eggs

Combining two southern favorites into one dish results in a treat few can resist.

MAKES 12

Pop the yolks out of each hard-boiled egg half and place them into a bowl. Mash the yolks with the back of a fork, then stir in the mayonnaise, salt, 1 teaspoon of the chives, roasted peppers and juice, and cheese. Spoon yolk filling into whites and top with the remaining chives.

6 hard-boiled eggs

1½ tablespoons mayonnaise

scant ¼ teaspoon kosher or sea salt

3 teaspoons finely minced fresh chives, divided

1 tablespoon minced jarred roasted red peppers plus 1 teaspoon juice

¼ cup finely shredded sharp cheddar cheese

Kale Chips 🍥

1 bunch kale

¼ cup olive oil or melted
   coconut oil

1 teaspoon ground turmeric

½ teaspoon garlic powder
   (not garlic salt)

Popcorn salt

Buying kale chips in the store is an expensive endeavor. I find it especially painful to part with my money for a bag of store-bought chips because they are so easy to make at home! The one and only downside is that your kitchen will smell a bit like cabbage—just open a window.

MAKES 8 SERVINGS

Preheat the oven to 300°.

Line a rimmed baking sheet with aluminum foil and spray with nonstick cooking spray.

Rip the kale leaves from their thick stems using your hands or a paring knife. Tear into large, chip-size pieces and lay them on the foil—do not overlap.

Drizzle the leaves evenly with oil and toss with your hands to coat each leaf, then season with turmeric, garlic powder, and very lightly with popcorn salt. You may need to bake the chips in batches or at the same time using multiple rimmed baking sheets.

Roast for 20 minutes, turn the baking sheet, and continue roasting for 15 minutes longer, or until crisp. Serve at once or allow to cool and keep in an airtight container for up to three days.

Soups, Stews, Broths, and Gravies

Why do we so love a warm bowl of stew or an ample ladle of gravy? We eat soup all year round in the South. Be it the dead of winter or blazing-hot summer, it doesn't matter: soup is a staple with no regard for season. All good soups, stews, and gravies start with a great broth; the little time it takes to make it pays off in spades.

Corncob and Leek Broth 🌱

6–8 corncobs (kernels
    removed)
2 medium leeks, washed
    well to remove sand,
    ends trimmed off
1 plump garlic clove, peeled

I try to use every bit of my ingredients, be they animal, vegetable, fruit, or even cheeses. Leftover bones from a roasted chicken makes an excellent stock; citrus skins zested and mixed with butter and garlic make a pungent topping for pasta; Parmesan cheese rinds add an umami blast to simmering soups; and corncobs simmered with leeks in salted water render a remarkably sweet and savory base for countless soups, stews, and sauces. It can stand in for chicken broth in most recipes, and it's virtually free to make—I *love* that!

MAKES 2–3 QUARTS

Lay everything into a big pasta pot and cover with 3 quarts (12 cups) of water. Cover and bring to a simmer, then crack the lid and allow to bubble away for 30 minutes. Strain out the cobs, leeks, and garlic, and the stock is ready to be seasoned as you like.

Roasted Vegetable Broth 🟤

The difference between stock and broth is that stock is generally made with bones, as in chicken or beef stock, which creates a rich, gelatinous liquid, whereas broth is made with meat or vegetables.

A good broth or stock is the foundation of many recipes. My default had always been chicken stock, full of silky collagen, but as soon as I developed this vegetable broth I became a convert. Roasting the vegetables creates a depth that will set up any recipe with savory results.

MAKES 7–8 CUPS

Preheat the oven to 400°.

Generously smear a rimmed baking sheet with 1 tablespoon of the oil, pile in the prepared vegetables, and drizzle the remaining oil over them, tossing to coat evenly.

Roast the vegetables, uncovered, in the preheated oven for 30 minutes. Remove from the oven and stir, pushing the vegetables from the edges into the middle, and vice versa. Place back into the oven and roast 30 minutes longer.

Scrape the roasted vegetables into a large stockpot, pour 1 cup of hot water into the roasting pan to get up any fond (brown bits stuck to the pan), and then pour this liquid into the stock pot. Add 8 more cups of hot water, miso paste, and tomato paste. Cover with the lid cracked and set over high heat. Bring to a strong boil, then reduce the heat to medium-low or low and simmer very gently for 30 minutes. Season with salt to taste. When the broth is done, strain out and discard the vegetables.

Keep refrigerated for up to a week or freeze for up to 3 months.

2 tablespoons vegetable oil, divided

½ large head green cabbage, chopped into chunks

1 large carrot, peeled, chopped into chunks

1 large yellow onion, chopped

2 large portobello mushroom caps, cut into quarters

2 celery stalks, trimmed and chopped into chunks

2 tablespoons blond miso paste, found in the international section of most grocery stores, or refrigerated

1 tablespoon tomato paste

1 teaspoon kosher or sea salt, more to taste

Chickpea Broth 🅥

Simmering the beans with an onion, garlic, and Parmesan rinds adds so much flavor to the beans and the broth. Parmesan rinds are an inexpensive way to add savory notes to almost any simmering liquid. Find the rinds in the fancy cheese section of most grocery stores.

MAKES 4–6 CUPS

Bring everything to a simmer over medium-high heat in a large, covered pot. Reduce the heat to low and crack the lid. Cook for about 90 minutes, until the beans are soft (this time will depend on the age of the beans—older beans take longer to soften). You may need to add a cup more of hot water to keep the beans amply submerged.

You can use the beans immediately or freeze them in a single layer, then pile the frozen beans into a zip-top freezer bag. They will keep for 3 months and are better than canned beans.

Strain out the onion, garlic, and Parmesan rinds, then store the broth in the refrigerator for up to a week or freeze for up to 3 months.

1 pound dried chickpeas

8 cups water

1 small yellow onion, peeled, left whole

3 plump garlic cloves, peeled, left whole

1 cup Parmesan cheese rinds

Senate Bean Soup 🄥

1 pound dried navy beans

1 medium yellow onion, chopped small

1 teaspoon tomato paste

3 tablespoons blond miso paste, found in the international section of most grocery stores or refrigerated

2 teaspoons kosher or sea salt

1 teaspoon liquid smoke

1 teaspoon smoked paprika

1 medium carrot, peeled and diced

2 celery stalks, trimmed and diced

1 medium baking potato

2 tablespoons vegan butter (such as Earth Balance)

Senate bean soup is served every day in the dining room of the U.S. Senate building. I don't care for politics, but I sure do love bean soup. This one is interesting because in addition to the usual suspects (beans, celery, carrots, and onions), mashed potatoes are incorporated—creating a creamy background for the smoky, savory beans. Speaking of smoky, this version of Senate bean soup is vegan—I've forgone the traditional smoked ham hock used to season the soup, replacing it with not only smoked paprika but also liquid smoke, both natural ingredients that are readily available at grocery stores. I've also amped up the umami with miso paste—don't skip it. This soup is so satiating and so hearty that you'll never miss the meat.

MAKES 6–8 SERVINGS

In a large soup pot, cover the beans with water by 3 inches. Bring to a boil and cook, covered, for 2 minutes, then turn the heat off, keep the pot covered, and allow the beans to sit in the hot water for an hour.

Drain and rinse the beans. Pile them back into the soup pot, pour in 10 cups of water, and add the onions. Cover and raise the heat to medium-high, bring to a strong simmer, then reduce heat to medium and gently simmer, uncovered, for an hour.

After an hour of simmering, the beans will have softened somewhat but not completely (this has to do with the age of the beans). Add the tomato paste, miso paste, salt, liquid smoke, smoked paprika, carrots, and celery to the pot, raise the heat to medium-high, return to a boil, and then reduce the heat to medium to keep the soup simmering steadily. Cook, uncovered, until the beans are soft, 30–60 minutes longer.

While the soup is simmering, make the mashed potatoes: Peel the potato and cut it into large chunks. Place the chunks into a small pot, cover with water, and season with a pinch of salt. Cover, set over high heat, and bring to a boil. Cook for 10–15 minutes,

··················
: 1 pound dried :
: beans equals   :
: 3–4 (15-ounce) :
: cans of beans :
··················

36

until the potatoes are easily pierced with the tip of a knife. Drain and use a fork or potato masher to mash the potatoes with vegan butter. Set aside.

Once the beans are as soft as you like, stir the mashed potatoes into the soup. Serve hot. This soup tastes even better the next day.

Umami Mushroom Broth 🕐

8 ounces white button or
   brown mushrooms,
   trimmed and quartered
   (stems intact)
½ ounce dried porcini
   mushrooms
1 large portobello
   mushroom cap, sliced
1 small yellow onion, sliced
   in half
1 tablespoon blond miso
   paste, found in the
   international section
   of most grocery stores,
   or refrigerated
2 teaspoons kosher or
   sea salt (if this is to be
   reduced into a sauce,
   omit the salt)

This broth is so versatile. I cook rice in it, make mushroom soup out of it, or reduce it down and finish it with truffle butter to make an addictive pasta sauce.

MAKES 4–6 CUPS

Place all the ingredients into a large pot, then pour in 8 cups of water. Cover and turn heat on to medium-high just to bring to a boil, then immediately crack the lid and reduce the heat to medium-low.

Simmer gently for an hour. Be aware that after an hour, a substantial amount of liquid will have evaporated. Use tongs to remove the mushrooms and onions from the broth (tossing them with a little butter and piled onto toast makes a nice snack). Carefully pour the broth from the pot, leaving behind the sediment at the bottom. Alternatively, pour the broth through cheesecloth that has been folded over a few times to catch the sediment (discard the cheesecloth).

Keep refrigerated for up to a week or freeze for up to 3 months.

Corn Bisque

This simple soup gives the corn a starring role. The bisque gets its flavor from fresh corn as well as Corncob and Leek Broth. Don't skip this broth—it's easy to make and adds depth to this dish.

MAKES 6–8 SERVINGS

Place the corn, potatoes, celery, and onions into a large saucepan or soup pot. Pour in the broth, cover, and bring to a simmer over medium-high heat. Crack the lid, reduce the heat to medium or medium-low, and simmer until the potatoes are very tender, about 10–15 minutes.

Purée the soup with an immersion blender, or transfer the soup to a stand blender and purée, pouring the soup back into the pot once smooth. Add the cream and bring to a low simmer, cooking gently for 2 minutes. Season with salt and serve at once.

3 cups fresh or frozen corn kernels
1 to 1½ pounds Yukon Gold potatoes, cut into ½-inch cubes (3 cups)
2 celery stalks, trimmed and chopped
1 medium yellow onion, chopped
8 cups Corncob and Leek Broth (page 32)
1 cup heavy cream
Kosher or sea salt, to taste

Monica Galloway

Georgia Peanut Soup

People are always surprised at how delicious this soup is. The peanut fragrance is more pronounced than the actual flavor. It's filling, warming, and elegant.

MAKES 6–8 SERVINGS

Heat the vegetarian chicken (or vegetable) broth over medium-high until simmering.

While you are waiting for the broth to heat, make the roux: Melt the butter in a large soup pot set over medium-high heat. Once it is frothy, add the onions and celery and cook until soft and fragrant.

Add the flour and stir well, reducing the heat to medium or medium-low. Cook, stirring often, until the roux smells nutty and turns golden, about 3–5 minutes. Add the simmering broth and tomato paste, whisking as you go. Increase the heat to medium-high, bring to a simmer, and cook for 10 minutes.

Once the soup has cooked for 10 minutes, turn off the heat and, using an immersion blender, purée the soup until smooth, then immediately add the peanut butter and use the immersion blender again to purée until smooth. Finish the soup by setting it over low heat and whisking in the half-and-half (or milk); taste and season with salt if desired. Do not let the soup simmer from this point on.

To serve, ladle into bowls and scatter the green onions and roasted peanuts over the top.

8 cups water

3 tablespoons Better than Bouillon's No Chicken Base (or vegetable bouillon cubes)

4 tablespoons (½ stick) unsalted butter, cut into pieces

1 medium yellow onion, chopped

2 celery stalks, trimmed and chopped

3 tablespoons all-purpose flour

1 heaping tablespoon tomato paste

2 cups natural (unsweetened) smooth peanut butter

1 cup half-and-half or whole milk

Kosher or sea salt, to taste

4 green onions, chopped

½ cup chopped roasted peanuts

Winter Tomato and Rice Soup 🌀

2 tablespoons olive oil

1 small celeriac (celery root), peeled and grated (2 cups)

1 medium carrot, peeled and roughly chopped

1 medium yellow onion, chopped

1 plump garlic clove, peeled and roughly chopped

1 (28-ounce) can plum tomatoes, with their juice

6 cups Roasted Vegetable Broth (page 33) or Chickpea Broth (page 35)

1 tablespoon tomato paste

1 tablespoon sambal oelek (spicy, chunky chili-garlic paste found in the international section of most grocery stores)

1 tablespoon fresh lemon juice

½ cup long-grain white or brown rice

My friend Monica is all about tomatoes. If I call her and say, "I've just made tomato sauce would you like s—," she interrupts shouting, "Yes! If it's tomatoes, I'm your girl!"

We get the most glorious tomatoes in the Carolinas from April to October. In the beginning of the season, farm stands bring ripe tomatoes up from Florida and they are fantastic, but toward mid-May, we see local tomatoes at farmers' markets and farm stands and they're outstanding. So, even though we only have to survive five months without ripe tomatoes, I wanted to come up with a tomato soup to satiate my friend's tomato dependence in the colder months.

This recipe uses canned tomatoes; try to get San Marzano tomatoes if you can. It's a satiating soup any time of year.

MAKES 8 1-CUP SERVINGS

Heat the oil in a large soup pot over medium heat. Once the oil is shimmering, add the celeriac, carrots, onions, and garlic. Sauté for 10 minutes until the celeriac and onions begin to caramelize (turn brown in spots), then add the tomatoes, refill the tomato can with the broth (swishing around to swirl up any remaining tomato juice), and pour into the pot, along with the tomato paste, sambal oelek, and lemon juice. Cover and bring to a simmer, reduce the heat to medium-low, crack the lid, and simmer gently for 15 minutes.

After 15 minutes, all the vegetables should be soft. Use an immersion blender to purée or transfer the soup to a stand blender and purée, pouring the soup back into the pot once smooth. Taste and season with salt, if desired.

Raise the heat to medium-high and pour in the rice. Cover and bring just to a simmer, then reduce the heat and cook gently until rice is cooked, about 15 minutes. Serve hot.

Tomato Essence Soup 🌱

A few summers ago, I was obsessed with savory popsicles and ice creams. Creamy smoked salmon with asparagus swirl and blue cheese with candied pecans were my favorite ice creams to make. My favorite popsicle was ripe tomato purée with sea salt and basil. I know, it sounds weird, but I just don't have a sweet tooth and wanted to enjoy frozen treats. Honestly, they were all divine.

The ripe tomato purée inspired this soup. It is easy to make and, other than salt, has only four ingredients. It is sublime. Make certain to use only super-fresh, ripe tomatoes, no hot house or gassed "vine-ripened." You'll find the best ones at farmers' markets and produce stands. This is a time to use expensive, fruity olive oil—it shines in this dish.

MAKES 3–4 CUPS

4 pounds fresh, ripe tomatoes, stems removed, roughly chopped (no need to remove seeds)

½ small shallot

1 small garlic clove

1 teaspoon kosher or sea salt

¼ cup extra-virgin olive oil

Pop everything except the olive oil into a food processor or blender and purée until smooth, about a minute.

Set a chinois, or fine metal strainer, over a large bowl and pour the tomato purée into the strainer. Push the purée into the strainer; the juice will flow through, leaving the pulp and seeds behind. Whisk this juice with the olive oil and serve at room temperature, or store in the refrigerator for up to a day. Don't worry if the soup separates after some time; just stir, and it will come back together.

Jambalaya

12 ounces vegan chorizo meat (not links), found refrigerated in most grocery stores

3 tablespoons vegetable oil, divided

1 large yellow onion, chopped

3 plump garlic cloves, microplaned or minced

1 green bell pepper, chopped

2 celery stalks, trimmed and chopped

½ teaspoon kosher or sea salt

1 small eggplant (about 1 pound), skin on, cubed (3 cups)

3 medium ripe tomatoes, chopped (3 cups)

1 tablespoon Cajun or Creole seasoning

3 cups Corncob and Leek Broth (page 32) or Roasted Vegetable Broth (page 33)

1½ cups long-grain white rice

Jambalaya is an excellent, affordable dish to serve a crowd. Rice stretches this intensely flavored stew into a filling meal, packed with colorful vegetables and spices. No need to tell people that it's vegan, just let them enjoy your wonderful dish—they won't miss a thing.

This recipe calls for vegan chorizo, rather than the classic andouille. I find that vegan chorizo is much easier to find in the grocery store and it comes as loose meat, rather than in links, so its flavors can more easily infuse the dish with spicy goodness.

MAKES 6–8 HEARTY SERVINGS

In a large Dutch oven, sauté the chorizo in 1 tablespoon of the oil over medium-high heat for 2–3 minutes. Add the remaining oil and pile in the onions, garlic, bell peppers, and celery. Add the salt and reduce the heat to medium. Cook, stirring often, for 5 minutes, then toss in the eggplant, tomatoes, and Cajun or Creole seasoning and stir well. Cover and continue cooking for 5 minutes longer.

Pour in the broth, raise the heat to medium-high, cover with the lid cracked, and bring to a strong simmer. Immediately pour in the rice and stir to distribute evenly. Cover again and bring to a gentle simmer, then lower the heat to medium or medium-low, keep the pot covered with the lid cracked, and cook for 20–30 minutes, until the rice has absorbed the broth and is tender.

Gumbo 🕐

The secret to any good gumbo is the roux—this is true whether you are making a meaty gumbo with duck, a seafood gumbo packed with shellfish, or a vegan gumbo full of vegetables like this one. The roux will dictate color, add tremendous flavor, and thicken the stew. Take the time to make a proper roux.

MAKES 6 SERVINGS

Pour the oil into a large soup pot and set over medium heat, then add the flour and stir with a wooden spoon or heat-proof spatula to combine well; it should look like wet sand. Stir every minute or so until you can smell it, then reduce the heat to medium-low or low and stir constantly until the roux becomes the color of an old penny—red-brown—this will take up to 25 minutes. Do not walk away from a cooking roux because it can burn very quickly and you'll have to start again.

When the roux is the right color, pile in the bell peppers, onions, celery, zucchini, okra, Cajun or Creole seasoning, and smoked paprika. Stir to incorporate the ingredients and cook, stirring every minute, for about 5 minutes.

Add the diced tomatoes and their juice and hot broth, stir, and raise the temperature to medium-high. Cover with the lid cracked, bring to a boil, then reduce heat to medium-low and simmer, with the lid cracked, stirring occasionally, for 20–30 minutes. Serve with cooked rice.

¼ cup vegetable oil

¼ cup all-purpose flour

½ red bell pepper, chopped

½ green bell pepper, chopped

1 medium yellow onion, chopped

1 celery stalk, trimmed and chopped

1 small zucchini, ends trimmed, the rest cut into quarter moons

½ pound fresh okra, trimmed and chopped (frozen may be substituted)

1 tablespoon plus 1 teaspoon Cajun or Creole seasoning

1 teaspoon smoked paprika

1 (14-ounce) can plain diced tomatoes, with their juice

4 cups hot Roasted Vegetable Broth (page 33)

"Chicken" and Dumplings 🌱

I learned from my Turkish friend Meltem that authentic hummus starts with dried chickpeas, never canned. It takes a little extra time but truly results in the most remarkable hummus.

When my youngest daughter joined her older sister in becoming vegetarian, I started to think more seriously about transforming their favorite southern meat dishes into vegetarian-friendly dishes; chicken and dumplings was one of their most requested dinners, so I started there.

Hummus and chicken and dumplings collided one day when, after pressure cooking chickpeas, I noticed that the water in which the beans cooked looked identical to a golden chicken stock—it even smelled the same! With a few aromatic additions, I was able to transform a liquid that I'd been throwing away for years into a comforting bowl of southern goodness that honestly tastes the same as the meat-filled classic.

MAKES 4 HEARTY SERVINGS

In a large soup pot, bring the first 7 ingredients to a simmer over medium-high heat, uncovered. Reduce heat to medium and simmer gently for 30 minutes (adding in ½ cup of water as the soup reduces).

Remove the bay leaf, onion, and celery and discard. Raise the heat to medium-high, cover, and bring the soup to a boil, then add the dumplings or noodles and cook according to package instructions until tender. If using fake chicken, add it now, and simmer gently for 5 minutes. Serve at once or store in the refrigerator for up to 3 days.

8 cups Chickpea Broth (page 35)
1 teaspoon poultry seasoning
2 tablespoons Better than Bouillon's No Chicken Base (optional)
½ teaspoon freshly ground black pepper
1 bay leaf
½ small yellow onion, not chopped
1 celery stalk, broken into 2 pieces
12–14 frozen dumplings (in the grocery's freezer section) or 2 cups broad egg noodles
8 ounces cubed imitation chicken (such as Quorn)
Kosher or sea salt, to taste

Roasted Cauliflower Étouffée 🌱

1 head cauliflower, broken
   into bite-size florets
¼ cup plus 2 tablespoons
   vegetable or light olive
   oil, divided
3 teaspoons Cajun or Creole
   seasoning, divided
2 large stalks celery,
   trimmed and diced
   (1 cup)
1 large green bell pepper,
   diced (1½ cups)
1 medium yellow onion,
   diced (1½ cups)
3 tablespoons all-purpose
   flour
1 (15-ounce) can fire-
   roasted diced tomatoes,
   with their juice
3 cups water
1 bunch green onions,
   chopped

Spicy, savory, and so comforting—étouffée is a classic Cajun stew of sorts that usually contains crawfish or shrimp. I've replaced shellfish with roasted cauliflower and it is a treat! Truly, you will never miss the seafood in this dish.

MAKES 6 SERVINGS

Preheat the oven to 450°.

Spray a rimmed baking tray with nonstick cooking spray, pile the cauliflower florets on, drizzle with 2 tablespoons of the oil, and sprinkle with 1 teaspoon of the Cajun or Creole seasoning. Toss and distribute the cauliflower evenly across the pan. Place in the oven and roast for 10 minutes, stir, and continue roasting for 5 minutes longer. Set aside.

Heat ¼ cup of the oil in a 2-quart (or larger) pot and set over medium-high heat. When the oil starts to shimmer, add the holy trinity (celery, green bell peppers, and onions). Sauté for about 5 minutes, until the vegetables are soft, then lower the heat to medium and sprinkle in the remaining Cajun or Creole seasoning and the flour. Stir well, evenly distributing the seasoning and flour. Cook for just a minute, as the pot will become dry.

Add the tomatoes and their juice and the water into the pot and stir well to scrape up the cooked-on bits from the bottom of the pan. Raise the heat to medium-high and bring the étouffée to a strong simmer, uncovered, then stir, lower the heat to medium, and simmer gently for 20 minutes. After 20 minutes, add in the roasted cauliflower, stir well, and serve with the green onions and long-grain rice.

Slow Cooker Green Tomato Chili 🌱

1–1½ pounds green tomatoes, chopped (4 cups)

2 pasilla peppers, chopped

1 large green bell pepper, chopped

1 plump jalapeño pepper, seeded and chopped

1 large baking potato, peeled and chopped

1 large yellow onion, chopped (1½ cups)

3 plump garlic cloves, minced

1 cup fresh or frozen corn kernels

2 heaping teaspoons ground cumin

½ teaspoon kosher or sea salt

1 tablespoon Better than Bouillon's No Chicken Base (or 2 large vegetable bouillon cubes)

2 cups chopped fresh cilantro, divided

1 cup beer (Budweiser, Pabst Blue Ribbon, or Corona work well)

1 heaping tablespoon finely ground yellow or white cornmeal

¼ cup water

1 (19-ounce) can cannellini beans, rinsed and drained

Shredded cheese

Sour cream

Freshly sliced jalapeño peppers

Chopped green onions

Corn chips

I knew that I liked my cousin's new husband when he made me a dish from his homeland of Peru. It was a simple chicken and rice dish, but it was exploding with flavor. I simply couldn't get enough of the combination of fresh cilantro and cumin! Flash forward a few decades, as our family began eating more plant-based meals: one of our favorite chilis was a chicken chili verde (green chicken chili). What made the dish so delicious was that cilantro-cumin combo—the chili was just as tasty without chicken. This is one of the few dishes that I make again and again—it's always a welcome dinner for my family and is so easy to make in the slow cooker.

If you can't find green tomatoes, tomatillos work just as well.

MAKES 6–8 SERVINGS

Place first 11 ingredients in a large (8-quart) slow cooker. Toss to distribute the cumin and salt evenly. Stir in 1½ cups of the cilantro, then pour in the beer. Cover and set the slow cooker to high. Cook for 4–6 hours.

During the last hour, smash the potatoes with a potato masher or the back of a fork. Mix together the cornmeal with water, then stir it into the chili along with the remaining cilantro and beans, cover again, and cook for the remaining hour.

Serve with sour cream, shredded cheese, jalapeños, green onions, and corn chips.

Brunswick Stew 🦃

Brunswick stew is claimed by Brunswick, Georgia, and Brunswick County, Virginia, as originating in both locales. It's essentially a tomato-based vegetable and meat stew. Which meat is used depends on which part of the South you are in. Squirrel or rabbit are what was historically most common, but Virginia recipes usually have chicken and rabbit, whereas Georgia versions tend to include pork and beef.

This version has none of those, relying instead on TVP, or textured vegetable protein, to go along with all those veggies. A few secret ingredients amp up the meaty flavor profile. Don't leave out the blond miso, tomato paste, or liquid smoke (which is a natural ingredient)—none are overt but all are invaluable to flavoring this stew.

MAKES 6–8 SERVINGS

Bring 1 cup of the broth to a boil, remove from the heat, and pour in the TVP. Stir, cover, and allow to sit until all the liquid is absorbed, a matter of minutes.

In a Dutch oven or very large, lidded pot, sauté the onions, bell peppers, garlic, and potatoes in the oil over medium heat for 5 minutes, then add the diced tomatoes and juice, corn, lima beans, remaining broth, liquid smoke, thyme, miso paste, tomato paste, and prepared TVP. Stir, cover, bring to a gentle simmer, and cook for 15 minutes on medium-low or low, then season with salt to taste.

2½ cups Corncob and Leek Broth (page 32), Roasted Vegetable Broth (page 33), or Umami Mushroom Broth (page 38), divided

1 cup TVP, found dried in most grocery stores and all health-food stores

1 small yellow onion, chopped

1 red bell pepper, chopped

2 plump garlic cloves, microplaned or minced

2 large red potatoes, cut into ½-inch cubes

2 tablespoons vegetable oil

1 (28-ounce) can diced tomatoes, with their juice

1 cup fresh or frozen corn kernels

1½ cups frozen baby lima beans

½ teaspoon liquid smoke

½ teaspoon ground thyme

1 tablespoon blond miso paste, found in the international section of most grocery stores, or refrigerated

1 tablespoon tomato paste

1–2 teaspoons kosher or sea salt

Tomato Gravy

The first time I had tomato gravy, I was in Asheville, North Carolina, at a little breakfast diner. It was so incredibly delectable that I couldn't stop thinking about it. As soon as I returned home, I developed a recipe for it, burning my tongue as I impatiently slurped up the simmering gravy.

Tomato gravy is about the best way to start a day. It's also fantastic over biscuits with sautéed spinach and a poached egg for dinner. The classic version starts with bacon drippings, but I've replaced that smoky goodness with smoked paprika and the silky mouth-feel with butter and cream cheese. This vegetarian version tastes like thick, creamy tomato soup—heavenly.

MAKES SLIGHTLY LESS THAN 2 CUPS

Heat the butter in a 2-quart saucepan over medium heat until it melts and froths, then add the onions, stir well, and reduce the heat to medium-low. Cook this way, stirring occasionally, for about 4 minutes, until the onions are soft and translucent, not at all colored (this is called sweating the onions).

Add the flour and stir well (this is now a roux, a thickening agent); cook gently for about 2 minutes, until it's fragrant and smells nutty.

Pour in the tomatoes and their juice, plus half a can (about 1 cup) of water, the salt, smoked paprika, and brown sugar. Raise the heat to medium and bring to a simmer, covered, then reduce the heat to medium-low or low, so that the tomatoes are barely bubbling, and then uncover and mash the tomato pieces with a fork. Cook, stirring often, for 5 minutes.

Just before serving, stir in the cream cheese; turn off the heat and cover to allow the cheese to melt. Stir and serve.

2 tablespoons unsalted butter

1 small yellow onion, diced (1 cup)

2 tablespoons all-purpose flour

1 (13.5-ounce) can plain diced tomatoes, with their juice

1 teaspoon kosher or sea salt

¼ teaspoon smoked paprika

½ teaspoon light brown sugar, packed

1 tablespoon cream cheese

Sawmill Gravy

4 tablespoons (½ stick) unsalted butter

1 medium-large yellow onion, finely minced (1¼ cups)

8 ounces vegetarian breakfast sausage (such as Morning Star Farms, Quorn, or Gimme Lean), thawed (if frozen), crumbled

¼ cup all-purpose flour

3 cups whole milk

2 tablespoons heavy cream

1 teaspoon kosher or sea salt

½ teaspoon dried sage

⅛ teaspoon ground thyme

Sawmill Gravy originated in the southern lumber camps, where cooks had to make a filling and economical breakfast for a hundred or more men. A full fry-up, with bacon, sausage, eggs, and biscuits, was out, but simple, hearty Sawmill Gravy was ideal. The gravy used only a few ingredients and no meat; it was made from just bacon drippings, flour, and milk.

In many parts of the country, what was once known as Sawmill Gravy is now referred to as sausage gravy, because rather than bacon drippings, ground breakfast sausage and its drippings are cooked in a thick, creamy gravy. It is delicious but a bit heavy. I've lightened up the dish by using vegetarian breakfast sausage, and I swear to you that 98 percent of people would never be able to tell the difference.

MAKES 4–6 SERVINGS

Melt the butter in a medium saucepan over medium-high heat. Add the onions, stir, and cook until soft, roughly 3 minutes. Reduce the heat to medium, add the crumbled breakfast sausage, and cook for 1–2 minutes.

Pour the flour into the pan and stir to combine (this is a roux). Cook for 2 minutes, then pour in the milk and cream. Use a whisk to combine the roux with the dairy.

Raise the heat to medium-high and keep whisking until the gravy begins just to bubble around the edge of the pan, then reduce the heat to medium-low, stirring often. Sprinkle in the salt, sage, and thyme and simmer very gently, uncovered, for about 5 minutes. Serve over Easy Drop Biscuits (page 168) or toast.

Herb Gravy 🌱

This gravy is so good you'll want to drink it. At least I did. It's every bit as good as beef or poultry gravy. Make sure to use Chickpea Broth; it is critical to this recipe.

MAKES 4 CUPS

Sauté the onions with vegan butter in a medium saucepan, set over medium heat, until the onions are soft, about 5 minutes. Sprinkle in the flour and cook, stirring often, for just a minute, then pour in the broth, raise the heat to medium-high, and bring to a simmer, stirring often. As soon as it simmers, reduce the heat to medium-low and cook, stirring occasionally, until the gravy thickens, about 5 minutes.

Stir in the fresh herbs, black pepper, and soy sauce. Taste and season with salt, if desired. For very smooth gravy, purée using an immersion or stand blender.

1 small yellow onion, minced (1 cup)

¼ cup vegan butter (such as Earth Balance) or vegetable oil

¼ cup plus 1 tablespoon all-purpose flour

4 cups Chickpea Broth (page 35)

1 teaspoon finely chopped fresh sage

1 teaspoon finely chopped fresh thyme

1 teaspoon finely chopped fresh rosemary

¼ teaspoon freshly ground black pepper

1 teaspoon soy sauce

Kosher or sea salt, to taste

"Beef" Gravy for Rice 🌱

1 large shallot, chopped
(¾ cup)

1 tablespoon vegan butter
(such as Earth Balance)
or vegetable oil

2 large portobello
mushroom caps,
chopped (2 cups)

½ large green bell pepper,
chopped (1 cup)

¼ teaspoon kosher or
sea salt

3 tablespoons all-purpose
flour

2 cups Umami Mushroom
Broth (page 38) or
Better than Bouillon's
No Beef base

1 tablespoon soy sauce

1 cup meatless beef
crumbles (such as
Beyond Beef), frozen
(*not* thawed)

Southerners love their gravies! We've got beef gravy, pork gravy, chicken gravy, white gravy, brown gravy, tomato gravy, even chocolate gravy. Gravy is appropriate (and appreciated) at practically every meal.

Back in the day, gravies were a great way of turning a small, inexpensive piece of meat into a flavorful main dish—a ladle of gravy over rice or a biscuit makes a satiating meal.

I've taken traditional beef gravy, which is thick enough to be a stew, and made it vegan by using both meaty mushrooms and vegetarian "beef" crumbles. If you don't have time to make Umami Mushroom Broth, you can use Better than Bouillon's No Beef Base—it's a vegetarian beef stock alternative that is equally appetizing.

MAKES 8 SERVINGS

In a large saucepan set over medium heat, cook the shallots in the vegan butter until they are soft, about 3 minutes. Add the mushrooms and bell peppers, season with salt, stir, cover with the lid cracked, and cook until the mushrooms release their liquid and the bell peppers are soft, 5–10 minutes, stirring occasionally.

When the liquid is released and the mushrooms still look wet, sprinkle in the flour, stir, and cook for about 2 minutes. Pour in the broth, soy sauce, and frozen beef crumbles, stir, and raise the heat to medium-high. Bring just to a simmer, reduce the heat to medium-low, and simmer gently for 5 minutes. Serve over long-grain rice.

Chocolate Gravy

You read that right, chocolate gravy. It's made with ingredients you'll probably have on hand and is a sweet morning treat spooned over biscuits. It's remarkably easy to make, with a texture crossed between pudding and chocolate syrup. Kids gobble it up, but chocolate lovers of any age will be thrilled to find a new way to work chocolate into their morning meal.

MAKES 2 ½ CUPS

Whisk everything except the butter together in a medium saucepan and cook over medium heat to a simmer. Whisk constantly as it thickens and bubbles for 2 minutes. Turn the heat off and whisk in the butter. Serve over warm biscuits.

¼ cup unsweetened cocoa powder

¼ cup all-purpose flour

¾ cup granulated sugar

Big pinch kosher or sea salt

2 cups whole milk

2 tablespoons unsalted butter

Hearty Main Dishes and Casseroles

Burgers, po' boys, fried "chicken," "crab" cakes, even barbecue—they're all here! Not to mention a cheesy broccoli bake that will make you swoon. No matter which recipe you prepare from this section, you'll never miss the meat!

Baked Nashville Hot Cauliflower

Hattie B's is a restaurant in Nashville renowned for its hot chicken. Nashville Hot Chicken is fried chicken that is brushed with spicy red oil as soon as the crisp pieces are pulled from the fryer.

I was in Nashville while on book tour for my first cookbook, *Learn to Cook 25 Southern Classics 3 Ways*, and insisted that our first stop be Hattie B's. I roped my dear friend and Nashville resident Rick into coming with me. At 11 a.m. there was already an hour-long line, just to get in. The wait was worth every minute. The chicken was crisp and well seasoned, and the sauce was stingingly spicy. It was the kind of food that I craved for months after having it.

Half a year later, as I was developing recipes for this book, I texted Rick to say that I was going to make a healthier vegetarian version of Nashville hot chicken and asked for his thoughts. "Why not cauliflower?" he replied. Brilliant, Rick is brilliant.

If you think about it, in many spicy chicken dishes, the poultry itself is more of a carrier of flavor than much of a flavor component itself, so cauliflower can easily stand in.

I chose to bake the cauliflower florets rather than frying them, and they turned out surprisingly well—crisp and golden outside, soft inside.

The hot sauce for Nashville Hot Chicken is traditionally made from oil in which the chicken has been fried. I replace that with melted butter for this recipe.

This dish would be equally as good sans hot sauce and drizzled with cheese sauce.

2½ cups crushed Ritz crackers (about 60 crackers)
1 cup buttermilk
1 large egg
1 large head cauliflower, broken into florets
Popcorn salt
Nashville Hot Sauce (recipe follows)

MAKES 6 SERVINGS

Preheat the oven to 400°. Spray a rimmed baking tray with nonstick cooking spray and set aside.

Place the cracker crumbs into a bowl. Whisk together the buttermilk and egg in a separate bowl. Dip a handful of cauliflower florets in the buttermilk and egg mixture, then toss the cauliflower into the cracker crumbs, coating them evenly. Place the breaded florets onto the prepared baking tray.

Bake for 15 minutes, turn each floret over, and bake for 10 minutes longer. Brush or drizzle the florets liberally with Nashville Hot Sauce as soon as they come out of the oven. Season with popcorn salt and serve immediately.

Nashville Hot Sauce

MAKES SLIGHTLY MORE THAN ½ CUP

In a small bowl, stir together the melted butter, cayenne (yes, it's 2 tablespoons), powdered sugar, salt, onion powder, and garlic powder. Serve warm.

8 tablespoons (1 stick) unsalted butter, melted

2 tablespoons cayenne pepper

1 tablespoon powdered sugar

1 teaspoon kosher or sea salt

½ teaspoon onion powder (not onion salt)

½ teaspoon garlic powder (not garlic salt)

Southern Fried Tofu Nuggets

2 (14-ounce) packages
    extra-firm tofu, drained

2 tablespoons light brown
    sugar

1½ tablespoons kosher
    or sea salt

1–2 cups vegetable or
    peanut oil, for frying

1 cup cornstarch

1 cup all-purpose flour

2 tablespoons baking
    powder

¼ cup powdered milk

2 teaspoons powdered
    sugar

1 teaspoon freshly ground
    black pepper

1 teaspoon poultry
    seasoning

2 large eggs, beaten

1 cup buttermilk

Popcorn salt

There are a few tricks to making tofu denser, chewier, and more flavorful. Soaking in boiling brine firms up and seasons the tofu. Dunking the tofu in a highly seasoned batter and frying gives it the same characteristics as southern fried chicken.

This recipe takes some time, but it can be done in stages. Brine the tofu the day before so all that's left to do is fry.

The craggy, golden crust and shape of Southern Fried Tofu looks like large chicken nuggets and has the crunch and poultry seasoning of classic fried chicken.

MAKES 6 SERVINGS

Slice each block of tofu into nugget-size pieces and place into a large casserole dish or bowl. In a saucepan, bring 4 cups of water to a boil, add the sugar and salt, and stir until dissolved. Pour the boiling water over the tofu pieces, making sure they are submerged. Soak the tofu in the hot brine for 15 minutes, then drain.

Line a baking tray with 2 layers of paper towels and lay the tofu pieces on top without overlapping them. Place 2 more layers of paper towels on top of the tofu, then place another baking tray on top. Place a few heavy cans, a pot, or heavy book on top of the baking tray and allow the tofu to be pressed for 10 minutes. You can do this up to a day ahead and store, covered in an airtight container, in the fridge.

Prepare to fry: Pour 1 inch of oil into a 10-inch cast-iron or other heavy skillet, cover, and set over medium heat. Preheat the oven to 300°. Have a clean rimmed baking tray ready.

Mix together the cornstarch, flour, baking powder, powdered milk, powdered sugar, black pepper, and poultry seasoning in a large bowl. Whisk together the eggs and buttermilk in a separate large bowl.

Toss several pieces of the tofu into the cornstarch and flour mixture until fully coated, shaking off excess. Place the coated tofu into the egg and buttermilk mixture and turn to coat. Drain

off the excess egg and buttermilk and place the tofu back into the cornstarch and flour, tossing to coat evenly.

Lay the coated tofu pieces into the hot oil and fry until golden on one side, about 2–3 minutes, then turn over and fry the other side until golden, 2–3 minutes longer. Place the fried pieces on baking trays, season them with popcorn salt, and keep warm in the oven as you fry the remaining tofu.

Charleston's Country Captain ⓥ

This dish shows up often in Charleston community cookbooks. It's essentially a tomato-based chicken curry. I've substituted tofu for the chicken; baking the tofu gives it a pleasing, chewy texture that mimics chicken. Traditionally, Country Captain starts with sautéing bacon. In order to keep this recipe vegan, I do away with the bacon but add smoked paprika and finish the dish with smoked almonds for a wonderful smoky background flavor and yummy crunch.

MAKES 6–8 SERVINGS

Preheat the oven to 400°. Spray a rimmed baking tray with non-stick cooking spray and set aside.

Drain the tofu and slice into 1-inch cubes. Dry the cubes with paper towels and pile onto the prepared baking tray. Drizzle with the oil and sprinkle 2 teaspoons of the curry powder over the cubes, then toss them gently. Arrange the cubes in the pan so that they aren't overlapping. Bake for 30 minutes, then remove from the oven, stir the cubes, and place them back into the oven for 15 to 30 minutes longer, until they are firm and golden. This step may be done up to a day ahead, the baked cubes sealed and stored in the refrigerator.

Set a large saucepan or Dutch oven over high heat and sauté the bell peppers, onions, and garlic in the vegan butter until soft, about 5–10 minutes, reducing the heat to medium-high if they begin to brown.

Add the tomatoes into the pan, then fill the tomato can halfway up with water, swirl to capture any tomato remnants, and add this to the pot. Add the salt, smoked paprika, raisins, and remaining curry powder. Stir and bring just to a simmer, then reduce the heat to medium-low, cover with the lid cracked, and cook gently for 15 minutes.

After 15 minutes, stir in the baked tofu. Cover with the lid cracked and simmer 15 minutes longer. Just before serving, stir in the green onions. Top each serving with a small handful of the chopped smoked almonds. Serve over long-grain rice or grits.

2 (14-ounce) packages super-firm tofu

2 tablespoons vegetable oil

5 teaspoons curry powder (spicy or mild—your choice), divided

1 green bell pepper, chopped

1 medium yellow onion, chopped

1 plump garlic clove, minced

2 tablespoons vegan butter (such as Earth Balance)

1 (28-ounce) can plain crushed tomatoes with their juice

1 teaspoon kosher or sea salt, more to taste

½ teaspoon smoked paprika

½ cup golden raisins

1 bunch green onions, chopped

1 cup smoked almonds, roughly chopped

Vegetable Purloo 🌱

2 tablespoons minced
shallot

2 plump garlic cloves,
microplaned or minced

1 medium yellow onion,
diced

3 tablespoons olive oil

2 cups long-grain rice

¼ pound fresh okra,
trimmed and sliced
(1 cup)

1 cup fresh or frozen
corn kernels

1 large tomato diced
(1½ cups)

4 cups Corncob and Leek
Broth (page 32)

1 bay leaf

1 teaspoon kosher or
sea salt

Purloo hales from the South Carolina Lowcountry and is very similar to pilaf in that both are rice dishes cooked with vegetables and usually meat or seafood. Cooking the okra, corn, and tomatoes in the rice allows all their flavorful juices to soak into the rice grains as they gently simmer.

MAKES 6 SERVINGS

In a Dutch oven or large lidded pot set over medium-high heat, sauté the shallots, garlic, and onions in the oil for 3 minutes, then reduce the heat to medium and add the rice. Continue sautéing for 5 minutes longer, stirring often. Stir in the okra, corn, and tomatoes, then add the broth, bay leaf, and salt, stir once, reduce the heat to medium-low or low, so that the broth is barely simmering, and cover. Simmer for 25–35 minutes, until all of the broth is absorbed and the rice is tender. Remove the bay leaf and serve.

Pulled "Pork" Barbecue 🥬

2 (17-ounce) cans green
    jackfruit in water or brine
    (*not* syrup), rinsed and
    well drained
3 tablespoons vegetable oil
2 tablespoons sweet
    paprika
½ teaspoon ground thyme
Dash of ground nutmeg
1 teaspoon ground cumin
1 teaspoon onion powder
    (not onion salt)
1 teaspoon garlic powder
    (not garlic salt)
1 teaspoon smoked paprika
½–1 teaspoon seasoned salt
    (such as Lawry's)
BBQ Sauce (recipe follows)

Barbecue in the South is a noun, not a verb, and always refers to pork . . . except in this case. Canned, green jackfruit mimics the texture of pulled pork. When doused in a tangy sauce and paired with coleslaw, it's honestly hard to tell the difference between the pork and produce versions.

Look for canned green jackfruit in water, never syrup, at Asian grocery stores (fresh green jackfruit won't work).

MAKES 4 HEARTY SERVINGS

Preheat the oven to 400°.

Pick through the drained jackfruit pieces, removing and discarding seeds, then shredding the rest by hand. The pieces should be chunky, not too finely shredded. Spray a rimmed baking tray with nonstick cooking spray and pile in the jackfruit. Drizzle with oil, then sprinkle with the spices and seasoned salt. Use your hands to toss and coat all the pieces evenly.

Roast for 20 minutes, toss the jackfruit pieces, and continue roasting for 20 minutes longer, then pour ¾ cup of the BBQ Sauce over, stir, and continue roasting for just 5 minutes longer. To serve, pile onto soft buns, drizzle with more BBQ Sauce, and top with coleslaw.

BBQ Sauce 🍅

1 cup ketchup

¼ cup molasses

2 tablespoons cider vinegar

1–2 tablespoons honey or
   agave nectar, to taste

2 teaspoons soy sauce

1 teaspoon liquid smoke

1 teaspoon Worcestershire
   sauce

½ teaspoon kosher or
   sea salt

MAKES SLIGHTLY MORE THAN 1 CUP

Whisk everything together and either simmer for 2–3 minutes or microwave for 1 minute.

"Crab" Cakes

I attended culinary school in Baltimore, Maryland, where I learned about picking blue crabs steamed in Old Bay seasoning. Picking crabs is as much about the act as it is about the eating. Friends or family sitting around a picnic table, wooden mallets and small metal picks in hand, cold cans of beer resting close by. This is a familiar summer memory for many Marylanders. It's also a lot of work prying that precious crabmeat from its sharp shells. What I love about crab cakes is the crispy exterior and soft interior filled with fresh vegetables like red bell peppers, celery, and corn, and of course Maryland's zesty seasoning blend, Old Bay.

Maryland is rightfully renowned for its crab cakes seasoned with Old Bay. Old Bay Seasoning is redolent of celery seed, dry mustard, clove, mace, and paprika. I use it in a lot of recipes, not just with crab.

In this recipe, crabmeat is replaced with hearts of palm, sometimes called swamp cabbage in the South. You may recognize hearts of palm from salads, but when shredded they look a lot like crabmeat. Flavoring the crab cakes with Old Bay, Dijon, and cracker crumbs makes them taste and look a lot like real crab cakes, and incorporating nori (toasted seaweed) adds a touch of sea flavor.

MAKES 8

Slice the hearts of palm into thirds, then roughly chop in thirds lengthwise, creating shreds that resemble crabmeat. Alternatively, pulse the hearts of palm in a food processor until just roughly chopped. Place into a large bowl.

Sauté the bell peppers, onions, celery, corn, and garlic in the butter over medium heat until just soft, about 5 minutes. Scoop the vegetables into the bowl with the hearts of palm and stir in

2 (14–15-ounce) cans hearts of palm, rinsed and drained

¼ large red bell pepper, minced (¼ cup)

½ small yellow onion, minced (¼ cup)

1 small stalk celery, minced (¼ cup)

¼ cup frozen corn kernels, no need to thaw

2 plump garlic cloves, microplaned or minced

1 tablespoon unsalted butter

½ cup minced fresh parsley

1 tablespoon very finely chopped nori (toasted seaweed, found in the international section of most grocery stores)

1 tablespoon plus 2 teaspoons Old Bay Seasoning, divided

1 teaspoon Dijon mustard

1½ cups crushed Ritz crackers (about 36 crackers), divided

½ cup mayonnaise

¼–½ cup vegetable oil, for frying

Pimento Aioli (page 155), for serving

the parsley, nori, 1 tablespoon of the Old Bay, mustard, ½ cup of the cracker crumbs, and mayonnaise. Stir well to combine, then cover and refrigerate for at least an hour and up to 4 hours.

When ready to eat, heat ¼ cup oil in a 10-inch cast-iron or other heavy skillet and form the "crab" mix into 8 patties. Toss the remaining cracker crumbs with the remaining Old Bay. Dredge the patties in the crumb mixture and fry 4 at a time until crisp and golden on one side, about 4–5 minutes, adding more oil to the pan if it becomes dry; then carefully flip them and fry the other side until crisp and golden. Serve with Pimento Aioli.

"Oyster" Po' Boys

With their mineral flavor and tender, chewy texture, fried oysters are a treat. I wanted to find a way to replicate them in vegetarian form for this classic New Orleans sandwich.

Preparing oyster mushrooms the same way traditional oysters are for po' boys is a revelation! The first time I made these, my kids fought over who got the last crunchy bite. Their flavor and texture are remarkably similar to the fried shellfish—they even look like the real thing.

MAKES 4

Look over the mushrooms: if they are in large clumps, slice them into smaller, oyster-size pieces. If they are large but singular, keep them whole.

Preheat the oven to 300°. Have a rimmed baking sheet at the ready.

Place a 10-inch cast-iron skillet or heavy-bottomed pan over medium heat and pour 2 inches of oil into the pan. Cover and heat.

While the oil is heating, make a breading station: Stir together the flour and cornmeal in a bowl. Whisk the eggs in a separate bowl.

When the oil is hot and ready for frying (the oil will shimmer and will sputter when a drop of water is flicked in), dip several mushrooms in the egg mixture until well coated, then toss them in the cornmeal mixture to coat. Place the mushrooms into the hot oil and fry for 5 minutes per side, turning only once, until golden brown. Remove from the oil, place on a baking sheet, and season with the popcorn salt, then place the baking sheet immediately into the oven to keep the mushrooms warm as you fry the rest.

When ready to serve, slice the rolls in half, spread with Mississippi Comeback Sauce or mayonnaise, lay in the lettuce and tomatoes, then heap the fried "oysters" in and eat at once.

1 pound oyster mushrooms

Canola, peanut, or vegetable oil, for frying

½ cup all-purpose flour

1 cup yellow or white cornmeal

4 large eggs

Popcorn salt

Hoagie rolls

Lettuce

Ripe tomato slices

Mississippi Comeback Sauce (page 134) or mayonnaise

Carolina Veggie Burger

While I was writing this book, my dear friend Michal asked me to open a burger restaurant for him. It was an interesting experience eating and writing mainly vegetarian while developing recipes for burgers. When I agreed to open the restaurant for Michal, I had two conditions: we would use only organic, humanely raised beef and we would offer many meat-free dishes, including a really good veggie burger.

The resulting veggie burger recipe is below. I was even asked to prepare this recipe on Headline News's *Weekend Express*—what a kick! I adore this burger, as do many of the customers at the burger restaurant. It is both hearty, due to the healthy fats from walnuts, and filling, due to the fiber in black beans, with a very meaty flavor from smoked paprika, miso paste, and Parmesan.

MAKES 4

Place the walnuts, half the black beans, garlic, paprika, green onions, tomato paste, miso paste, Parmesan, salt, and egg into a food processor and pulse to form a chunky paste.

Remove from the food processor and stir in the remaining beans and cooked quinoa. Cover and refrigerate for 1 hour.

Form the mixture into 4 patties. Pour a few teaspoons of oil into a cast-iron skillet or heavy sauté pan and set over medium heat. Place the patties in, making sure not to crowd the pan, and cook for about 5 minutes, until a nice crust forms on the bottom. Spoon a bit of oil on top of each patty and carefully flip them over. Reduce the heat to medium-low and cover with the lid cracked. Cook the other side for about 5 minutes. Serve as you would a meat burger—with buns, cheese, lettuce, tomato, and condiments.

¾ cup walnuts

1 (15-ounce) can black beans, rinsed and drained, divided

2 plump garlic cloves, peeled and trimmed

½ teaspoon smoked paprika

4–5 green onions, chopped

1 teaspoon tomato paste

1 teaspoon blonde miso paste, found in the international section of most grocery stores, or refrigerated

½ cup grated Parmesan cheese

¼ teaspoon kosher or sea salt

1 large egg

½ cup cooked quinoa, at room temperature

Vegetable oil, for griddling

Slow Cooker BBQ Cabbage Rolls

FOR THE CABBAGE ROLLS

1 cup Roasted Vegetable
    Broth (page 33) or
    Chickpea Broth (page 35)

1 cup TVP, found in most
    grocery stores and all
    health-food stores

1 small yellow onion,
    chopped (½ cup)

1 tablespoon unsalted
    butter

2 cups cooked long-grain
    rice

2 large eggs

½ teaspoon seasoned salt
    (such as Lawry's)

8 large green cabbage
    leaves

FOR THE BBQ SAUCE

1 (28-ounce) can plain
    crushed tomatoes

½ cup dry white wine

¼ cup light brown sugar,
    packed

1½ teaspoons kosher or
    sea salt

1½ tablespoons cider
    vinegar

1 teaspoon liquid smoke

Our friend George was raised in Canada by his Ukrainian mother and father, who still call him by his given name, Uri. George grew up speaking Ukrainian and eating his mother's fantastic pierogis and stuffed cabbage. He's lived in the American South so long now that he eats Ukrainian food only when his mother comes to visit and he speaks Ukrainian only after a couple glasses of wine (he's very entertaining that way). I thought George would appreciate this dish more than anyone, so I asked his wife, Aimee, to test it. Aimee reported back that she and the kids loved the dish but that George said, "I'm Ukrainian. Stuffed cabbage shouldn't have barbecue sauce." Old habits die hard.

TVP, or texturized vegetable protein, is an amazing meat replacement. It's fat-free, low in sodium, and a good source of fiber, with more protein than meat—it's extremely affordable to boot. You can find it in the baking aisle of many grocery stores and virtually all health food stores.

Use TVP for texture, not flavor—it has none. Like rice or tofu, TVP picks up the flavors that are added to it, so when rehydrating it, always use a flavorful liquid, then layer in more flavors as you cook.

TVP is most commonly found in a form that is best suited to replace ground meat, so it is great for making tacos, Bolognese sauce, shepherd's pie, and chili. It works beautifully in this recipe for cabbage leaves rolled around rice and "beef," then slowly braised in a light barbecue sauce in the slow cooker.

MAKES 8

Bring a large pot of water to boil for the cabbage leaves.

In a separate saucepan, bring the broth to a boil, remove from the heat, and add the TVP. Stir to combine and set aside to hydrate.

Sauté the onions in the butter over medium heat just until soft. Set aside to cool.

When the TVP, rice, and onions are cool, whisk the eggs, mix all together, and stir in the seasoned salt.

Drop the cabbage leaves into the boiling water, cover, and remove from the heat. Allow the leaves to sit, covered, in the hot water for 10 minutes.

Make the BBQ sauce by stirring together all of the ingredients. Pour a third of the BBQ sauce into a slow cooker, set on high, and cover.

Remove the leaves from the water individually to stuff and roll. Spoon ¼ cup of the TVP and rice mixture onto one end of a soft cabbage leaf, then fold the sides over and roll the leaf up. Place each roll, seam side down, in the slow cooker. After all the rolls are in the slow cooker, pour the remaining BBQ sauce on top, cover, and cook on high for 4–6 hours or on low for 6–8 hours.

Don't worry if the leaves rip a bit. They will be folded over and will hold the filling just fine.

Three-Cheese Broccoli Bake

8 cups broccoli florets,
    from about 2–3 heads
    broccoli

1 tablespoon kosher or
    sea salt

1 plump garlic clove,
    peeled and halved

1 tablespoon unsalted
    butter

1½ cups half-and-half

3 large eggs

¼ cup all-purpose flour

½ cup grated Parmesan
    cheese

½ teaspoon kosher or
    sea salt

½ teaspoon freshly ground
    black pepper

3 green onions, chopped

4 ounces Velveeta, cut into
    1-inch cubes

1 cup shredded sharp
    cheddar cheese

1 cup crushed Ritz crackers
    (about 24 crackers)

This is a classic crowd pleaser! Using three cheeses brings three different savory flavors to this dish. Cutting Velveeta into cubes creates puddles of gooey goodness oozing from between broccoli florets, and the crumb topping adds a nice crunch.

MAKES 6–8 SERVINGS

Preheat the oven to 375°.

Fill a large pot with very hot water and add the salt. Cover, set over high heat, and bring to a boil. When the water reaches a rolling boil, add the broccoli florets, stir, cover with the lid cracked, and return to a boil. Start timing when the water boils: cook for just 2 minutes, then drain and set aside.

Rub a 2-quart baking dish generously with the garlic half (this is a trick I picked up while living in Switzerland—the Swiss rub garlic on the inside of fondue pots to impart a delicate garlic flavor), then rub the dish with the butter and set aside.

Make the custard: In a large bowl, whisk together the half-and-half, eggs, flour, Parmesan, salt, and black pepper. Set aside.

Toss the broccoli with the green onions and layer into the prepared baking dish. Nestle the Velveeta cubes in among the broccoli florets, then whisk the custard again and pour over the broccoli. Scatter the cheddar over the top and finish by pouring the cracker crumbs evenly from edge to edge.

Cover with aluminum foil and bake for 25 minutes, then uncover and bake for 20 minutes longer (if cracker crumbs start to get too golden, re-cover with foil). Serve hot.

Cheddar Corn Pudding

3½ tablespoons unsalted
    butter, melted, divided
1½ cups half-and-half or
    whole milk
3 large eggs
1 teaspoon kosher or
    sea salt
1 teaspoon granulated sugar
2 tablespoons all-purpose
    flour
2 cups fresh or frozen corn
    kernels, thawed
4–5 green onions, chopped
1 cup shredded sharp
    cheddar cheese

This is a delicate corn side dish emboldened by sharp cheddar and green onions. Though not traditional, these two ingredients add oomph to the dish.

MAKES 6–8 SERVINGS

Preheat the oven to 350°. Grease a 9 × 13-inch baking dish with 1 tablespoon of the melted butter. Set aside.

    Whisk the half-and-half or milk, remaining melted butter, eggs, salt, sugar, and flour together until smooth. Stir in the corn, green onions, and cheddar. Pour the mixture into the prepared baking dish and bake uncovered for 35–45 minutes, until there's no jiggle in the middle. Serve hot.

Tomato Pudding

My mother and father both attended culinary school when they were fifty years old. They had been lifelong foodies (before that was a word), but they took cooking to a more serious level when they flew to Paris for the summer to study the art of cookery.

When my father tested this recipe for me, he phoned and said, "We used to eat this in college in the 1950s. We called it Train Wreck. I love this dish!" Although I liked his story, I didn't care too much for the name, so I stuck with the more traditional Tomato Pudding.

It is truly an old-school dish, said to have roots in the Great Depression kitchen. It's extremely economical and uses just a few staple ingredients.

Even though it's called a pudding and has sugar, this is served as a side dish. I've pulled back on the traditional whole cup of granulated sugar, using instead half a cup of brown sugar. It's still fairly sweet, but the unconventional addition of blue cheese balances that with a pleasing saltiness. For a sweeter, classic version of Tomato Pudding, feel free to omit the blue cheese.

MAKES 6–8 SERVINGS

8 tablespoons (1 stick) unsalted butter, melted, divided

8 cups freshly sliced bread cubes

1 (28-ounce) can plain crushed tomatoes, with their juice

½ teaspoon dry mustard powder

¼ teaspoon ground cinnamon

Scant dash ground cloves

1 teaspoon kosher or sea salt

½ cup light brown sugar, lightly packed

2–3 ounces blue cheese, crumbled

Preheat the oven to 350°.

Grease a 9 × 13-inch baking dish with 1 tablespoon of the melted butter. Pile the bread cubes into the buttered baking dish, pour the remaining melted butter over, and toss to coat.

Stir together the tomatoes and juice, mustard powder, cinnamon, cloves, salt, and sugar. Pour the mixture over the bread, but do not stir.

Place the baking dish in the oven, uncovered, and bake for 30 minutes, then remove from the oven, stir, and scatter the blue cheese crumbles on top. Continue baking for 30 minutes longer. Serve hot.

Cheese Grits Casserole

4 cups water

4 cups whole milk

2 hefty teaspoons kosher or
sea salt

½ teaspoon red pepper
flakes, more to taste

2 cups stone-ground yellow
or white grits

5 tablespoons butter,
divided

½ teaspoon garlic powder
(not garlic salt)

3 cups shredded sharp
cheddar cheese, divided

3 large eggs, beaten

1 cup grated Parmesan
cheese

The aroma of this dish alone is enough to incite pandemonium.
It's cheesy, soft cornmeal goodness—wonderful comfort food!
Great for a gathering, as well as just for the family, and perfect
on a holiday table.

MAKES 10–12 SERVINGS

In a large uncovered saucepan, bring the water, milk, salt, and red
pepper flakes to a boil over medium-high heat. Add the grits in a
slow, steady stream, stirring constantly with a wooden spoon or
heat-resistant rubber spatula. Once the grits are added, continue
stirring for 2 minutes (to prevent lumps), reduce the heat to low,
and cook, uncovered; the grits should not be simmering but rather
softly belching—a bubble bursting at the top every few seconds
or so. Continue cooking, stirring occasionally, until the grits are
soft and creamy, 30–40 minutes.

Preheat the oven to 350°. Grease a 9 × 13-inch baking dish with
1 tablespoon of the butter and set aside.

When the grits are soft and creamy (be careful, they will be
very hot), remove from the stove and stir in the garlic powder,
the remaining butter (cut into pieces), and 2 cups of the cheddar. Stir until the butter and cheese have melted. Allow to cool
off the heat, stirring every few minutes, for 10 minutes. Taste
and adjust seasoning (more salt or red pepper flakes?). Stir in
the beaten eggs, incorporating them well. Pour everything into
the prepared baking dish and top with the remaining cheddar
and the Parmesan. Bake, uncovered, until golden and smelling
outrageously delicious, 45–60 minutes. Let sit out of the oven for
15 minutes before serving.

Savory Pies

Savory pies seem historic to me, harkening back
to colonial days. It's amazing what roasted vegetables,
cheese, and eggs encased in tender piecrust can
accomplish—a sublime, simple meal.

All-Purpose Pie Dough

2½ cups all-purpose flour,
    sifted

1 teaspoon kosher or
    sea salt

1 teaspoon granulated sugar

12 tablespoons (1½ sticks)
    unsalted butter, frozen

8 tablespoons all-vegetable
    stick shortening (such as
    Crisco), frozen

6–8 tablespoons ice water

This pie dough works well for sweet or savory pies. It can be made up and frozen until needed or used as soon as it's rolled out.

MAKES 2 DISKS

Mix the flour, salt, and sugar together in a mixing bowl. Use a box grater to grate the frozen butter and shortening into the flour mixture. Rub the fats into the flour mixture until it resembles crumbs or coarse cornmeal, with a few pea-size lumps of floured fat. Incorporate the ice water (just the water, not the ice), 1 tablespoon at a time, into the dough mixture, stirring until the dough just comes together, ultimately adding about 6 tablespoons. Squish a small piece of dough between your fingers; if it sticks together, you've added enough water, but if it crumbles apart, add more water, 1 teaspoon at a time.

Turn the dough out onto a clean surface and shape into 2 disks. Wrap in plastic and refrigerate until ready to use, or place in a zip-top freezer bag and freeze for up to 3 months.

Ribbon Pie

You know those friends who, even when you haven't seen each other for years, you pick right back up with where you left off? I feel so fortunate to have many such friends. Our family has moved so often that we have friends all over the world. Although we stay in touch via email and texts, it's always a treat to see those who are dear to us in person.

Lisa has been my friend since middle school. We got in trouble in high school together, got married around the same time, had our first babies a month apart—we grew up together. Because of many kids and busy lives, Lisa and I have seen each other in person only a handful of times in the past fifteen years, but when she heard I was writing another cookbook, she offered to test recipes for me. And so we connected again, this time through food.

The trick to this stunning pie is using a vegetable peeler to turn the veggies into colorful ribbons—the slices must be very thin for them to wrap evenly. Keep in mind that beauty takes time. Allow 45 minutes to assemble, then 45 minutes (hands-free) baking time—it's absolutely worth the effort.

MAKES 8 SLICES

Preheat the oven to 375°. Remove the pie dough from the refrigerator.

Use a vegetable peeler to slice thin "ribbons" from the vegetables. You will not be able to use all of each vegetable, so you will have leftover scraps. You should end up with 3–4 cups of ribbons from each type of vegetable. Try and get a bit of the vegetable's colorful skin with each slice you take. Keep the vegetable slices separate; don't mix them together.

Mix together the mayonnaise, wine, Pecorino Romano, onions, and mozzarella.

Roll out the pie dough to about a ¼ inch thick and lay into a 9-inch deep-dish pie plate. Scoop the mayonnaise mixture into the bottom of the pie and evenly push it to the edges with the back of a spoon. Scatter the thyme over the mayonnaise mixture.

1 disk All-Purpose Pie Dough (page 92) or other prepared pie dough

4–5 medium orange or purple carrots, sliced (4 cups)

1 medium eggplant, sliced (3 cups)

2 medium zucchini, sliced (3 cups)

2 medium yellow squash, sliced (3 cups)

1 cup mayonnaise

1 tablespoon white wine

3 tablespoons grated Pecorino Romano cheese

2 tablespoons grated yellow onion

1 cup shredded mozzarella cheese

1 tablespoon fresh thyme

1½ tablespoons olive oil

Pinch of kosher or sea salt

PRO TIP

Use a microplane to purée the onions.

Take a carrot slice and roll it in a tight coil, then, still holding the coil in your hand, wrap a zucchini slice (skin-side up) tightly around the carrot coil. Place this carrot and zucchini coil in the center of the pie and continue wrapping the rest of the vegetable slices around the original coil. Use contrasting colors to make a strong impact (for example, orange next to green next to yellow next to purple). Continue this until the pie shell is filled with vegetable ribbons. Drizzle with the olive oil and scatter the salt over the top.

Bake in the preheated oven, uncovered, for 45 minutes. The vegetables should be crisp-tender when finished. Allow the pie to sit at room temperature for 15 minutes before (snapping pictures and then) slicing.

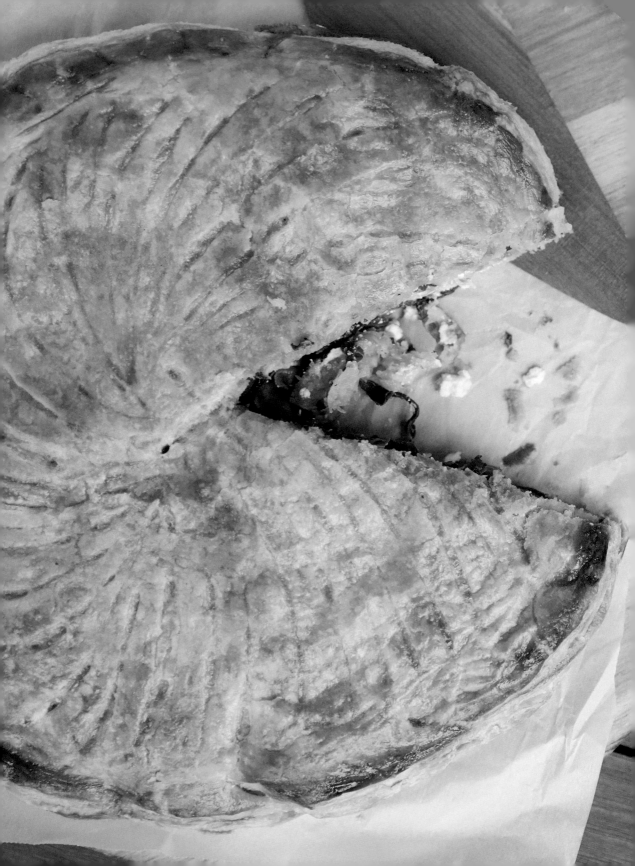

Vegetable Stuffed Pie

This savory pie makes quite an impression—it's so pretty! I love the oddity of its dome shape, and it's lovely when sliced open. Using frozen puff pastry is one timesaving trick, and cooking the butternut squash in the microwave is another way of making this dish a keeper.

Classically, this type of domed, stuffed pie is called a pithivier (pronounced *pith-i-veeyay*) and is thought to have originated in Pithivier, France. Although it's often made with a sweet almond paste filling, it works really well with sautéed greens and leeks, naturally sweet butternut squash, and tangy goat cheese.

MAKES 8 SLICES

Preheat the oven to 375°.

Remove the puff pastry from the freezer and thaw according to package directions.

Trim the top and bottom off of the butternut squash, then carefully cut the squash in half from top to bottom. Scoop out and discard the seeds. Place one half of the sturdy squash, cut side down, on a microwave-safe plate and microwave at full power for 5 minutes. Insert the tip of a sharp knife into the skin side of the squash: if it slides in easily, it's sufficiently cooked, but if there is resistance, microwave for 5 minutes longer. Depending on the size of the squash and the power of your microwave, this could take anywhere from 5 to 15 minutes—cook in 5-minute intervals until tender. Allow the cooked squash to cool, then slice off the skin and cut the squash into approximately 5 × 1-inch rectangles.

You will only use half of a large squash, more of a small one. Allow the squash to cool completely.

While the squash is microwaving, cook the leeks and Swiss chard or spinach. Melt the butter or olive oil in a large cast-iron skillet or a heavy sauté pan over medium-high heat, then add the leeks and ¼ teaspoon of the salt. Sauté until the leeks are just soft, adjusting the heat if needed. Add the Swiss chard or spinach to the pan and season with ¼ teaspoon more of the salt, then turn the greens so that they're on the bottom of the pan, leeks on top.

2 sheets (1 box) frozen puff pastry

1 small or ½ large butternut squash

2 tablespoons unsalted butter or olive oil

2 medium leeks, tender white part only, chopped and washed well

¾ teaspoon kosher or sea salt, divided

1 bunch Swiss chard or spinach, leaves only, washed and chopped (about 6 cups packed)

½ teaspoon ground turmeric

1 (4-ounce) log chèvre (goat cheese), crumbled

1 large egg

Stir in the turmeric and sauté, stirring often, until the greens are fully wilted and soft, about 5 minutes. Pull the pan off the heat and allow the vegetables to cool completely.

Unfold 1 puff pastry sheet onto a rimmed baking sheet lined with parchment paper or aluminum foil. Invert a 9-inch plate or bowl on the pastry and use a paring knife to cut around it, creating a 9-inch disk. Lay the butternut squash rectangles in the middle of the pastry disk, leaving a 1-inch border, clear of filling. Now scatter the crumbled chèvre on top of the squash. Press the cooked and cooled leeks and greens with a spoon or rubber spatula to squeeze out excess juices (leaving the juices in the pan) and mound the leeks and greens on top of the chèvre.

Unfold the other puff pastry sheet and invert the same 9-inch plate on it, but this time cut the disk 1 inch larger.

Brush the border of the bottom pastry with water, then drape the larger pastry disk over the vegetables and press the 2 disks together, crimping the dough as you go. Whisk the egg with 1 tablespoon of water and brush that over the pie. Use a sharp paring knife to cut a small cross at the top of the dome to allow steam to escape, then, starting at the cross, score lines down the pastry (you're not cutting through the pastry, just decorating it).

Bake 40–50 minutes, until the pastry is golden. Allow it to cool for 10 minutes before slicing. Serve warm or at room temperature.

Vidalia Onion and Clemson Blue Pie with Pecan Pretzel Crust

This is one of those dishes that people rave about; it tastes out of this world! A salty pretzel crust with sweet onions and tangy blue cheese—the combination is unbeatable.

MAKES 8 SLICES

To make the crust, place the pecan halves in a food processor and pulse 3 times for 3 seconds each time. Add the pretzels and pulse 3 more times for 3 seconds each, then add the brown sugar and salt and pulse for about 15 seconds, until the pecans and pretzels are ground into crumbs. Pour into a large bowl and stir in the melted butter. Use clean hands to mash the mixture, combining the butter with the crumbs evenly.

Spray a 9-inch spring-release pan with nonstick cooking spray and pile in the buttered crumbs. Push the crumbs evenly along only the bottom of the pan, then use a small drinking glass to compact the buttered crumbs even tighter. Place the pan in the freezer for 30–60 minutes.

Preheat the oven to 350°.

To make the filling, melt the butter in a large cast-iron skillet set over medium heat. Add the onions, stir, cover, and cook for 5 minutes (without stirring). Remove the lid and stir, sprinkle with the salt, and continue to cook the onions, uncovered, for about 10 minutes longer, until they are very soft and are beginning to color slightly.

Remove from the heat and add the crumbled blue cheese; it should melt in the residual heat of the onions. Set aside to cool completely.

Once the onions are cooled, mix with the beaten eggs and pour into the frozen pretzel and pecan crust. Bake, uncovered, for 25–35 minutes, until the center is just cooked. Remove from the oven and allow to cool at room temperature for at least 15 minutes before slicing. This dish is also really tasty served cold.

FOR THE CRUST

1 cup pecan halves

2 cups bite-size pretzels (not the sourdough type)

1 tablespoon light brown sugar

1 teaspoon kosher or sea salt

6 tablespoons (¾ stick) unsalted butter, melted

FOR THE FILLING

1 tablespoon unsalted butter

2 large Vidalia onions, sliced thin (8 cups)

1 teaspoon kosher or sea salt

3–5 ounces blue cheese, crumbled (Clemson blue if you can get it)

2 large eggs, beaten

Roasted Vegetable Potpie with Cream Cheese Peppercorn Crust

FOR THE CRUST

2 cups all-purpose flour

1 teaspoon kosher or
    sea salt

½ teaspoon freshly ground
    black pepper

16 tablespoons (2 sticks)
    chilled unsalted butter,
    cubed

8 ounces (1 block) chilled
    cream cheese, cubed

1–4 teaspoons ice water

FOR THE FILLING

2 cups small broccoli florets

1 large carrot, peeled and
    cut into ¼-inch rounds

1½ cups cubed, peeled
    celeriac root, or
    celery slices

1 small yellow onion,
    chopped

¾ cup fresh or frozen corn
    kernels

1 large red potato, cubed

4 ounces button or cremini
    mushrooms, trimmed
    and quartered

2 tablespoons light olive
    or coconut oil

½ teaspoon kosher or
    sea salt

This potpie is so satiating, no one, I mean no one, will ever miss the meat. Roasting intensifies the vegetables' depth and natural sweetness. The crust is a knockout—full of flavor in its own right. If at all possible, make this potpie with Umami Mushroom or Roasted Vegetable Broth—it is so worth the little extra effort.

I use celeriac root in potpie because I love the density and intense celery flavor. If you can't find celeriac (also called celery root) or don't want to fuss with peeling and trimming it, just use regular celery.

MAKES 8 SLICES

To make the crust, place the flour, salt, and black pepper into the work bowl of a food processor, pulsing a few times to mix. Add the cold butter and cream cheese cubes and pulse several more times, until the mixture looks like cornmeal, then pulse and add ice water 1 teaspoon at a time until the dough just comes together into a ball. Remove dough to a lightly floured surface and form into 2 equal-size balls. Flatten the balls into disks, wrap in plastic wrap, and refrigerate for at least an hour and up to a day.

To make the filling, preheat the oven to 425°.

Spray a rimmed baking tray with nonstick cooking spray and pile in all of the vegetables, distributing them evenly across the pan. Drizzle with the oil, toss to coat, and season with salt. Roast the vegetables for 15 minutes, stir, and roast for 10 minutes longer. Remove from the oven and scrape the vegetables and any fond (the yummy brown bits) on the bottom of the pan into a large mixing bowl. Set the vegetables aside to cool.

To make the gravy, melt the butter in a small saucepan set over medium heat. Once it is melted and frothy, add the flour; you are making a blond roux. Stir; it should look like wet sand. Keep stirring until you can smell the roux—it should smell buttery and slightly nutty—this takes about 3–5 minutes.

Stir in the poultry seasoning, then whisk in the broth, raise the heat to medium-high, and whisk often, until the gravy simmers and begins to thicken. Simmer gently, whisking every minute or so, for 5 minutes. Remove from the heat and pour over the vegetables in the mixing bowl, stir well to incorporate, then place in the fridge to chill completely.

To assemble the pie, preheat the oven to 375°.

Make the egg wash by whisking the egg with 1 teaspoon of cool water. Set aside.

Remove 1 dough disk from the fridge. Lightly flour a work surface and rolling pin and roll the dough out into a circle, ¼ inch thick. Lay the pie dough on the bottom of an ungreased, 9-inch deep-dish pie plate. Gently press the dough into the corners and against the sides of the plate. Trim the dough off the lip of the pie plate.

Spoon the fully chilled vegetables and gravy into the pie dish. Roll out the second dough disk like the first one. Lay the dough over the top of the vegetables and crimp to seal the edges. Cut a small cross in the middle of the potpie (this allows steam to escape as the pie bakes). Brush the pie with the egg wash and bake for an hour. Check the pie halfway through. If the crust's edges are browning quickly, make a collar by lightly affixing a 2-inch strip of aluminum foil around the edge of the pie.

Remove from the oven and allow to cool for 10 minutes before slicing.

FOR THE GRAVY

2 tablespoons unsalted butter

3 tablespoons all-purpose flour

¼ teaspoon poultry seasoning

2 cups Roasted Vegetable Broth (page 33) or Umami Mushroom Broth (page 38)

Kosher or sea salt, to taste

FOR ASSEMBLY

1 large egg

1 teaspoon cool water

Crunchy Tomato Pie

16 sheets (½ box) frozen
phyllo dough (such as
Athens)

½ cup olive oil, divided

2 pounds fresh, ripe
heirloom tomatoes

Kosher or sea salt, to taste

1 (8-ounce) container whole
milk ricotta

1 (4-ounce) log chèvre
(goat cheese)

2 tablespoons chopped
fresh herb of choice
(such as tarragon, basil,
or parsley)

1 bunch green onions,
chopped

Southern tomato pie is classically made with pie dough, ripe tomatoes, onions, mayonnaise, and cheese—it is divine! I wanted to add a crispy texture to the classic dish, so I have replaced pie dough with frozen phyllo dough. Phyllo dough is made up of paper-thin sheets of dough layered with either butter or oil—in this case, I chose olive oil. It bakes up crispy and crunchy with soft, oven-roasted tomatoes inside and the fresh flavors of creamy ricotta, chèvre, and herbs.

MAKES 8 SLICES

Preheat the oven to 350°.

Remove the phyllo dough from the freezer to thaw in its plastic sleeve, according to the package directions.

Spread 2 tablespoons of the oil on a rimmed baking tray. Cut the tomatoes into ½-inch slices and place on the baking tray (trying not to overlap them, but it's not the end of the world if they do). Season with salt and roast for 1 hour—your house will smell divine!

Remove the tomatoes from the oven and place a towel or a heatproof cutting board under one end of the baking tray, thus tipping the pan slightly to collect the yummy juices and flavored oil, which will be incorporated into the ricotta mixture. Raise the oven temperature to 375°.

Stir together the ricotta, chèvre, chopped herbs, and 1–2 tablespoons of that yummy roasted tomato juice and oil mixture. Taste and season with a bit of salt. Set aside.

Use a pastry brush to brush a 9-inch deep-dish pie plate with oil. Next, prepare the phyllo dough. Have a damp (not wet) kitchen towel ready, remove the phyllo dough from its plastic sleeve, unroll the dough, and lay it flat; cover the dough with the damp towel (the phyllo will dry out in minutes). You will be using 4 sheets of phyllo per layer. Take 2 sheets and lay into ½ of the pie dish, so that it drapes up and over the rim. Now do the same with 2 more sheets on the other side of the pie dish. Brush all the phyllo, including

the overlapping, with oil. Give the pie dish a ¼ turn and repeat the oil-brushing process. After each oiled layer goes down, give the dish a ¼ turn. You will have 4 layers.

Pile the green onions into the bottom of the pie and season them with a bit of salt, followed by the roasted tomatoes and the ricotta mixture. Finally, bring the phyllo dough that is draped over the sides of the dish up and over the pie to enclose it. Brush the very top with oil and grind some fresh black pepper over the top.

Bake in the preheated oven for 45 minutes, until the pie top is golden and crunchy. Allow the pie to rest for 10 minutes before slicing.

Vegetables and Side Dishes

These are the fun foods—the dishes that can change the trajectory of a potluck or take a family gathering and turn it into a feast of flavors. From bold and crunchy, like Fried Okra served with Mississippi Comeback Sauce, to soft and warming, like a bowl of Pimento Mac and Cheese, these recipes are sure to please.

Creamy Stovetop Mac and Cheese

1 pound medium shells
  pasta
1 (12-ounce) can evaporated
  milk
2 large eggs
1 tablespoon cornstarch
1 teaspoon seasoned salt
  (such as Lawry's)
½ teaspoon garlic powder
  (not garlic salt)
½ teaspoon onion powder
  (not onion salt)
1 teaspoon Dijon mustard
1 pound American cheese,
  cut or shredded into
  small pieces
8 ounces sharp cheddar
  cheese, shredded
4 tablespoons (½ stick)
  unsalted butter, cut
  into pieces

This is over-the-top creamy and cheesy. I use two types of cheese here: sharp cheddar for an intensity and zing and American cheese for a smooth and creamy sauce. Evaporated milk is real dairy milk from which 60 percent of the water has been evaporated, leaving behind a distinct dairy flavor. For easier shredding, buy a big piece of American cheese from the deli counter.

MAKES 6–8 HEARTY SERVINGS

Set a large pot of salted water over high heat, covered. Once boiling, add the pasta shells and re-cover. When the water returns to a boil, take the lid off, stir the pasta, and start timing, cooking uncovered for 8 minutes.

While the pasta is cooking make the sauce: In a large mixing bowl, whisk together the evaporated milk, eggs, cornstarch, seasoned salt, garlic powder, onion powder, and mustard, then scatter in the shredded cheese and stir until evenly incorporated into the sauce. Set aside.

After 8 minutes of boiling time, the pasta shells should be just al dente. Drain and immediately return the pasta to the pot, and add the butter. Set the pot over low heat and stir until the butter is melted, then add the cheese sauce and stir. Continue stirring every 20 seconds until all the cheese has melted and the sauce is cooked and creamy. Serve at once.

Cheesy Garlic Bread Stuffed Potatoes

I developed these potatoes to taste like cheese garlic bread—soft, cheesy, and garlicky on the inside with a crunchy crumb topping. They are great as either a main course or a fancy side dish.

MAKES 8

Microwave the potatoes: Place 2 pierced potatoes at a time on a microwave-safe plate and zap in the microwave for 10 minutes (less time for just 1 potato). After 10 minutes, squeeze the potatoes: they should yield easily to your fingers. If they're not soft, zap again in 3-minute intervals. Continue with the other pair of potatoes.

Preheat the oven to 375°.

After all the potatoes are microwaved, use a kitchen towel or hot pad to hold them, then slice them in half lengthwise. Scoop out the cooked potato, leaving the skin intact. Don't worry if the skin tears a bit—we can fix that later. Mash the potatoes with the raw garlic, 4 tablespoons of the butter, and salt, then add the sour cream and milk. Mash until smooth, then stir in the chives and mozzarella and stir to combine.

Evenly mound the mashed potato and garlic mixture into each potato skin, then flatten the tops. Here's where you can fix torn skins: mold the filling into the skin, and the potato will hold that shape when baked. Place the stuffed potatoes on a rimmed baking tray and scatter crouton crumbs evenly over all 8 halves. Melt the remaining butter and spoon over the crumb topping, then bake for 15 minutes, until the tops are golden. Serve at once with a tossed green salad, and dinner is done.

4 large baking potatoes, pierced several times with a fork

2 plump garlic cloves, finely minced or pressed

8 tablespoons (1 stick) unsalted butter, divided

½ teaspoon kosher or sea salt

½ cup sour cream

½ cup whole milk

¼ cup chopped fresh chives

2 cups shredded mozzarella cheese

1 cup crushed garlic croutons

Salted Caramel Bourbon Pecan Sweet Potato Soufflé

Southerners like their sweet potato dishes to be sweet, just like their tea. This is a ridiculously flavorful, decadent recipe. It's like having a side dish of dessert with dinner. The sweetness is complemented by a last-minute sprinkling of crunchy salt flakes and pecans.

MAKES 8 SERVINGS

Pierce each sweet potato several times with the tip of a sharp knife. Microwave them together in a microwave-safe dish for 10–15 minutes. Check after 10 minutes to see if all the potatoes are soft; if some aren't, remove the ones that are, turn the others over, and keep cooking. Allow them to cool, then scoop the cooked flesh from the skins, place them into a large bowl, and mash. Stir in the sweetened condensed milk, nutmeg, cinnamon, vanilla, salt, brown sugar, and 4 tablespoons of the melted butter. Once the sweet potato mixture is cool, stir in the beaten eggs.

Preheat the oven to 350°.

Grease a 6-cup baking dish with the remaining melted butter and pour in the sweet potato mixture. Cover with aluminum foil and bake for 30 minutes. Uncover, scatter the pecan pieces over the top, and continue to bake, uncovered, for 30 minutes longer (total cooking time is 60 minutes). While that's baking, make the bourbon caramel sauce.

Place the granulated sugar, water, and a pinch of salt into a heavy, medium-size saucepan. Do *not* use a small saucepan, because when the cream is added to the caramelized sugar, it will be very hot and froth up considerably; you don't want it to bubble over the sides of the pan. Bring the sugar water to a boil over medium-high heat, stirring often. As soon as it reaches a boil, stop stirring and reduce the heat so that the sugar mixture is strongly simmering, with lots of rambunctious but controlled bubbles. The sugar will turn pale yellow, then golden light brown; it will change very fast, so pay attention, and remember: no stirring. As soon as the sugar turns golden light brown, add the cream at once and stir vigorously. The sauce will go from lumpy to smooth

2½ pounds sweet potatoes

½ cup sweetened condensed milk

⅛ teaspoon ground nutmeg

¼ teaspoon ground cinnamon

1 teaspoon vanilla extract

½ teaspoon kosher or sea salt

½ cup light brown sugar, lightly packed

5 tablespoons unsalted butter, melted, divided

2 large eggs, beaten

1 cup chopped pecans

½ cup plus 1 tablespoon granulated white sugar

¼ cup water

½ cup heavy cream

1 tablespoon bourbon

1 teaspoon vanilla extract

½ teaspoon sea salt flakes (such as Maldon)

as it heats. Allow it to simmer for 5 minutes longer—no stirring needed, but you may if you like—then remove from heat and stir in the bourbon and vanilla.

When the sweet potato soufflé is done, remove from the oven and pour all of the bourbon caramel sauce over the top. Finish with the sea salt flakes. Serve hot or at room temperature.

Beans and Greens 🌱

I adore greens of all sorts—collards, kale, Swiss chard, mustard—they're all healthy and savory. This is a rather Italian way to prepare greens, because of the addition of a lot of garlic and white beans. The ripe tomato and a bit of vinegar bring balance to the dish. Serve it with crusty bread or over grits to soak up the juices.

MAKES 8 SERVINGS

Pour the olive oil into a large cast-iron skillet or Dutch oven, set over medium heat, and add the chopped garlic and red pepper flakes. Stirring constantly, cook for 3–5 minutes, until the garlic is very fragrant but not at all browned.

Add the chopped greens and turn so that the garlic is on top and the greens are beneath—they will reduce in volume significantly as they cook. Cook until the greens are bright green, then pour in the broth and cook, stirring occasionally, uncovered for 5 minutes. Add the white beans, tomatoes, and salt and simmer for 5 minutes longer. Finish with the vinegar, stir well, and serve.

3 tablespoons olive oil

1 head garlic, microplaned or minced

½–1 teaspoon red pepper flakes

12 large collard leaves (about 8 cups chopped and packed)

1 cup Chickpea Broth (page 35)

2 (15-ounce) cans white beans (such as cannellini, garbanzo, or great white northern), rinsed and drained

1 large, ripe tomato, chopped (about 1 cup)

1 teaspoon kosher or sea salt

3 teaspoons cider vinegar

Company Succotash

This is a dish I make when hosting a casual dinner party. It can be easily prepared in advance and popped in the oven before dinner, freeing the cook to tend to other dishes or chat with guests. It's a lovely dish—use an oven-safe glass baking dish if possible to show off the pretty vegetable layers.

MAKES 8 HEARTY SERVINGS

Preheat the oven to 350°.

Spray a rimmed baking tray with nonstick cooking spray and lay in the tomato slices. Season with salt and roast for 30–45 minutes, until soft.

While the tomatoes are roasting, sauté the garlic and onions with 2 tablespoons of the butter in a large cast-iron skillet set over medium heat. Cook until the onions are soft, about 2–3 minutes, then add the remaining butter, season with ¼ teaspoon of salt, and sauté, stirring every 2 minutes, until the corn softens, about 8–10 minutes.

Remove the tomatoes from the oven and raise the temperature to 375°.

Spray a 9 × 11-inch baking dish with nonstick cooking spray. Lay half of the tomatoes in the dish, then pile in the cooked lima beans and season lightly with salt. Next, pile in the garlicky onions and corn, top them with the other half of the roasted tomatoes, and finish by drizzling with the heavy cream.

Roast, uncovered, for 30 minutes. Serve hot.

2 pounds fresh, ripe tomatoes, cut into ½-inch slices

Kosher or sea salt

3 plump garlic cloves, microplaned or minced

1 medium yellow onion, chopped

3 tablespoons unsalted butter, divided

3 cups fresh or frozen corn kernels

12 ounces frozen baby lima beans, cooked according to package directions

¼ cup heavy cream

Old-School Buttermilk Mashed Potatoes

2 teaspoons kosher or
  sea salt, plus more
  for seasoning
8 large baking potatoes
1 cup buttermilk
8 tablespoons (1 stick)
  unsalted butter,
  cut into chunks

My father makes the best mashed potatoes. This is for two reasons: first, for eighty-four years he has used butter with wild abandon, especially in mashed potatoes, and second, he takes his time and uses the right equipment for the job—a ricer.

A ricer is a hand-held press that pushes potatoes through a metal plate with small holes in it, resulting in super-smooth mashed potatoes. An added benefit of the ricer is that there's no need to peel the potatoes; the skins delicately flavor the potatoes as they cook and slip off in the ricing process. If you don't mind lumps, just use a potato masher (as I often do), but if you want silky-smooth mashed potatoes, use a ricer.

MAKES 6–8 SERVINGS

Fill a large pot with water and add the salt.

If you aren't using a ricer, peel the potatoes, then cut them into thirds and place them in the water. If you are using a ricer, there is no need to peel the potatoes; just cut them into thirds and place them in the water. Cover the pot and place over high heat. Bring to a boil, then lower temperature to medium or medium-low, crack the lid, and simmer strongly until the tip of a sharp knife slides easily into the center of the largest potato chunk, roughly 15–20 minutes.

While the potatoes are cooking, pour the buttermilk into a small saucepan and add the chunks of butter. Set the pan over medium-low heat, just to melt the butter and warm the milk—do *not* allow the milk to boil or simmer.

Drain the cooked potatoes well; it's important that no water remains behind. If using a ricer, pile the hot cooked potatoes back into a dry cooking pot and rice the potatoes, a few chunks at a time, into a large bowl. Once all the potatoes are riced, stir in the warm buttermilk and butter and season with salt. If mashing with a potato masher, pile the hot potatoes back into the dry cooking pot and mash, adding the warm buttermilk and butter as you go; season with salt.

Serve at once, while the potatoes are very warm.

Crisp Broccoli and Smoked Almond Salad

8 cups broccoli florets, from
    2–3 large heads broccoli
1 cup mayonnaise, regular
    or vegan
3 tablespoons cider vinegar
3 tablespoons maple syrup
3 tablespoons finely minced
    shallot
½ teaspoon kosher or
    sea salt
½ teaspoon smoked paprika
¾ cup dried, sweetened
    cranberries
½ cup chopped smoked
    almonds

This is my favorite broccoli salad. I made it for my aunt Judy's eightieth birthday dinner. Judy is my mother's sassy, funny, younger sister (she would definitely want me to emphasize "younger"). I just adore her and was so glad to host her and her equally witty husband, Frank, at our house for the celebratory gathering. Everyone loved this salad—meat eaters and vegans alike.

Dried cranberries add a beautiful, contrasting color to this dish. Smoked paprika and smoked almonds replicate the flavor profile of smoky bacon. I've also replaced the traditional sugar in this with maple syrup, which tastes fabulous! This is a wonderful vegetarian or vegan recipe that will take pride of place on any table.

MAKES 8–10 SERVINGS

Place the broccoli florets into a large salad bowl and set aside. In a separate bowl, make the dressing by whisking together the mayonnaise, vinegar, maple syrup, shallots, salt, and smoked paprika. Pour the dressing over the broccoli and toss to coat evenly, then add the cranberries and almonds and toss again. Cover and chill at least 1 hour but up to a day before serving.

Winter Creamed Corn

Creamed corn is the most amazingly delicious dish when prepared with sweet summer corn, but our family gets a hankering for it in the colder months, too. I developed this recipe for the winter months using ingredients easily kept at hand.

MAKES 6–8 SERVINGS

Melt the butter in a large saucepan over medium heat. Once melted, add the frozen corn and salt, stir to coat with the butter, and cover and cook for 15–20 minutes, stirring every 5 minutes. The frozen corn will release liquid and steam in its own juices.

Once the corn is just tender, scoop 1½ cups out from the pan and place into a food processor or blender with the half-and-half, flour, and sugar. Process for 30 seconds, scrape down the sides, and process again for 10 seconds.

Pour the puréed corn back into the cooking pot and cook, stirring occasionally, for 10 minutes longer. Taste and adjust the seasoning with more salt or sugar if desired. Serve warm.

4 tablespoons (½ stick) unsalted butter

1 (2-pound) bag frozen corn, *not* thawed

1 teaspoon kosher or sea salt

½ cup half-and-half

1 tablespoon all-purpose flour

2 teaspoons granulated sugar

Individual Crunchy Mac and Cheese

1 pound uncooked elbow
macaroni, small shells,
or corkscrew pasta

7 tablespoons unsalted
butter, divided

¼ cup plus 1 tablespoon
all-purpose flour

2 cups whole milk

⅛ teaspoon garlic powder
(not garlic salt)

2½ teaspoons Cajun or
Creole seasoning

¼ teaspoon freshly ground
black pepper

1 teaspoon Dijon mustard

3 cups shredded sharp
cheddar cheese

1–1½ pounds fresh, ripe
tomatoes, seeds
squeezed out, flesh
chopped (about 3 cups)

1½ cups panko

½ cup freshly grated
Parmesan cheese

I'm not sure what inspired me to throw fresh tomatoes into this mac and cheese, but I'm glad I did: it is a juicy addition! The ripe tomato chunks play nicely off the creamy cheese sauce. Using Cajun spice to season the sauce adds a lot of flavor with very little heat—don't skip it.

MAKES 8 HEARTY SERVINGS

Preheat the oven to 350°.

Cook the pasta 1 minute less than directed on the package. Coat 8 small ramekins or a 2–4-quart baking dish with nonstick cooking spray and set aside. While the pasta cooks, make the cheese sauce.

Melt 4 tablespoons of the butter in a large saucepan set over medium heat. Once the butter is frothing, add the flour, lower the heat to medium-low, and stir often for 5 minutes, until it smells nutty but is still blond (you are making a roux, a thickening agent).

Raise the heat to medium and whisk in the milk. Cook, whisking often, until bubbles begin to form on the edges of the pan, then watch the heat—it may need to be adjusted higher or lower, so that the sauce is just barely bubbling, not simmering, as it thickens.

Once the sauce is thickened, add the garlic powder, Cajun or Creole seasoning, black pepper, and mustard and stir to combine, then return to a gentle bubble. Pile in the cheddar and lower the heat to medium-low. Cook, stirring often, until the cheese just melts, then remove the pan from the heat and stir in the tomatoes.

Cover and allow the sauce to rest off the heat for 5 minutes, then, in a large mixing bowl, pour the sauce over the cooked pasta and combine well.

In a separate pan, melt the remaining butter and stir in the panko and Parmesan.

Fill the prepared individual ramekins or the baking dishes with the mac and cheese and top with the buttered crumb topping. Bake for 30–45 minutes, until the top is golden and crunchy.

Dirty Rice

The traditional star of this dish is chicken livers, but I've come up with a few tricks to bring layers of flavor without meat. Cooking the vegetables slowly until they caramelize is one way. Stirring the finished rice with butter adds decadence, and tossing the rice with chopped green onions and parsley brings freshness.

MAKES 8 SERVINGS

Place a large cast-iron skillet or heavy sauté pan over medium heat and add the oil. When the oil is shimmering, add the holy trinity (celery, bell peppers, and onions) and give the skillet a shake so that the vegetables are evenly distributed, then sprinkle over the Cajun or Creole seasoning. Allow the holy trinity to cook for 15–20 minutes, uncovered, stirring every 2 minutes, until the vegetables begin to caramelize (turn brown) and the pan becomes dry.

Once the vegetables are soft and caramelized in spots, add the frozen "beef" crumbles and stir to combine. Pour in ½ cup water and stir to get up any fond (tasty brown bits of food stuck to the bottom of the skillet). Allow the vegetable mixture to bubble away until the water is almost evaporated, about 2 minutes. Then toss in the cooked rice and butter and stir well to combine. When the butter has melted into the rice, stir in the green onions and parsley. Serve at once.

1 tablespoon vegetable or light olive oil

2 stalks celery, trimmed and chopped (about 1 cup)

½ large green bell pepper, chopped (about ¾ cup)

1 small yellow onion, chopped (about 1 cup)

3 teaspoons Cajun or Creole seasoning

1 cup meatless beef crumbles (such as Beyond Beef), frozen (*not* thawed)

½ cup water

4 cups cooked long-grain rice

2 tablespoons unsalted butter

1 bunch green onions, chopped

½ cup chopped fresh parsley

Savannah Red Rice ⑰

2 tablespoons vegetable oil

1 green bell pepper, diced

1 red bell pepper, diced

1 medium red onion, diced

3 plump garlic cloves,
    microplaned or minced

1 teaspoon smoked paprika

½ teaspoon kosher or
    sea salt

2 cups long-grain rice

1 (28-ounce) can plain
    crushed tomatoes

1 cup Roasted Vegetable
    Broth (page 33) or
    Chickpea Broth (page 35)

5 dashes hot sauce (such
    as Tabasco)

Southern red rice is similar in many ways to Mexican red rice—both cook the rice in crushed tomatoes or tomato juice. Savannah red rice is the southern style in that the bell peppers and rice are usually cooked in bacon. I won't lie, it *is* pretty good, but cooking everything in vegetable oil and seasoning the dish with smoked paprika creates an equally tasty side dish—it's healthier and so pretty, too.

MAKES 8 HEARTY SERVINGS

Preheat the oven to 350°.

Set a large, oven-safe Dutch oven over medium heat and add the oil. When the oil is warm, add the bell peppers, onions, and garlic. Stir and cook, uncovered, until the vegetables begin to soften, about 5 minutes.

Add the smoked paprika and salt, then stir in the rice, coating the rice grains in the vegetable juices and oil.

After 1–2 minutes, pour in the crushed tomatoes, broth, and hot sauce. Cover and set into the preheated oven. Cook for 45 minutes, stirring once after 20 minutes. Serve hot or warm.

Brown Rice with Mushrooms 🌱

Simmering white rice in beef stock with mushrooms is how southerners make brown rice. I wanted to replicate that color and the rich flavor while making this a vegan dish. My rule about cooking vegetarian and vegan is that the final dish must be mouthwatering—if it's not, the recipe is deleted and I start over. This dish hits that mark: it's not glaringly vegan, just a scrumptious rice dish that happens not to contain anything from an animal.

MAKES 4 SERVINGS

Sauté the mushrooms and garlic with oil in a medium saucepan set over medium-high heat for about 3 minutes, then reduce the heat to medium-low or low. Season the mushrooms with the salt and gently sauté until they release their liquid, roughly 5 minutes longer.

Once the liquid is released, pour in the broth, cover with the lid cracked, and turn up the heat to medium-high. As soon as it comes to a strong simmer, pour in the rice, stir, and re-cover but watch carefully. When it returns to a simmer, immediately reduce the heat to medium-low or low, keep the pan covered, and cook for about 30–45 minutes, until the rice grains are soft. Check occasionally to make sure that the rice is gently bubbling. Serve hot or at room temperature.

4 ounces button mushrooms, cleaned, trimmed, and sliced

2 plump garlic cloves, microplaned or minced

1 tablespoon vegetable oil

¼ teaspoon kosher or sea salt

2½ cups Umami Mushroom Broth (page 000)

1 cup brown rice

Cauliflower "Rice" with Fresh Herbs 🖤

1 large head cauliflower

2 tablespoons vegetable oil or oil of choice

½–1 teaspoon kosher or sea salt

¼ cup chopped fresh cilantro (fresh basil, tarragon, or dill weed would be nice alternatives, too)

¼ cup chopped fresh chives

The Lowcountry was once known for the superior rice produced on its plantations. Rice remains as much an important part of a Lowcountry meal as grits. Our family adores white rice with any dinner—soft and seasoned with soy sauce or firm and glistening in butter, we want that in our bellies!

Cauliflower "rice" is a sublimely simple dish that replicates the look and texture of white rice with loads more nutrients and about one-quarter the carbohydrates of white rice, although our family eats it because it tastes great.

MAKES 4–6 SERVINGS

Preheat the oven to 425°.

Break the cauliflower head into large florets, about the size of your fist, and remove and discard (or compost) leaves. Using the largest holes on a box grater, grate the florets; do not grate the stems (discard or compost).

Spread the oil evenly on a rimmed baking tray, then evenly pile on the grated cauliflower "rice." A few layers of tiny cauliflower pieces is fine. Season with salt and roast in the preheated oven for about 20 minutes, until just starting to get golden in spots.

Remove from the oven and toss with fresh herbs. Serve at once.

Hoppin' John

Black-eyed peas thrive in the heat of the South. We're lucky to find fresh black-eyed peas at produce stands and farmers' markets around here, but they can be found dried everywhere and frozen in many parts of the country (canned lack the toothsome texture for which black-eyed peas are prized).

Hoppin' John is loved all year round, but it is a mainstay on the southern New Year's Day table alongside collard greens—the greens represent dollars and the black-eyed peas symbolize coins, both ensuring prosperity for the new year.

I left the rice out of this version (if you want it, just add cooked rice when the peas are done), and I replaced the ham hock typically found in Hoppin' John with a creamy sprinkling of shredded smoked Gouda. This is a hearty vegetarian option.

MAKES 8–10 SERVINGS

Pick through the peas, removing out any debris. Cover them by 3 inches of water in a stockpot, bring to a boil, and cook, covered, for 2 minutes, then turn the heat off, keep the lid on, and allow to sit for 1 hour.

Drain and rinse the peas, then return them to the pot. Add the miso paste and an onion half, then add the broth—it should cover the contents of the pot. Cover, set over medium-high heat, and bring to a simmer. Crack the lid, reduce the heat to medium-low, and simmer very gently until the peas are tender—anywhere from 45 to 90 minutes (older black-eyed peas take longer to soften). Replenish the pot with more broth or water as needed to keep the peas just barely covered. Be careful not to let the peas get mushy.

While the peas are simmering, chop the remaining onion half. Melt the butter over high heat, and add the bell peppers, jalapeños, and garlic, and cook until soft, about 5–7 minutes, then season with the salt.

Remove the onion half from the tender peas and stir in the cooked vegetables and green onions. Taste and season with salt and hot sauce, if desired. Spoon into a serving dish and cover with the Gouda. Serve at once.

1 pound dried black-eyed peas

4 cups or more Corncob and Leek Broth (page 32), Roasted Vegetable Broth (page 33), or Chickpea Broth (page 35)

1 tablespoon blond miso paste, found in the international section of most grocery stores, or refrigerated

1 large yellow onion, halved

2 tablespoons unsalted butter

1 green bell pepper, chopped

1 small jalapeño pepper, seeds and membrane trimmed out, the rest minced

2 plump garlic cloves, microplaned or minced

¼ teaspoon kosher or sea salt, plus more for seasoning

1 bunch green onions, chopped

Hot sauce (such as Tabasco), to taste

4 ounces smoked Gouda cheese, shredded (about 1½ cups)

Baked Limpin' Susan 🌱

½ pound fresh okra,
  sliced into ¼ inch coins
1 small yellow onion,
  chopped
1 medium jalapeño pepper,
  chopped (use seeds and
  membrane if you want
  a spicy dish, otherwise
  discard)
3 plump garlic cloves,
  microplaned or minced
1 tablespoon vegetable oil
½ teaspoon kosher or
  sea salt
2 cups chopped fresh,
  ripe tomatoes (about
  1 pound)
3½ cups Corncob and
  Leek Broth (page 32) or
  Roasted Vegetable Broth
  (page 33)
2 cups long-grain rice

The story goes that Limpin' Susan was Hoppin' John's wife. All I know is that it's a colorful rice and okra dish that even okraphobes will love; cooking okra with rice cuts down significantly on the pod's slime factor. Often the dish includes fresh shrimp, but I think it's equally good with just ripe tomatoes and fresh okra.

Baking is a great, hands-free way to prepare rice. The grains come out slightly softer than steaming or boiling rice, but the flavor is just as good, if not a little better.

MAKES 8 SERVINGS

Preheat the oven to 400°.

Sauté the okra, onions, jalapeños, and garlic in the vegetable oil, over medium-high heat, in an oven-safe Dutch oven or large, lidded pot. Cook until the onions are just soft, about 5 minutes.

Season with the salt, then add the chopped tomatoes and broth and raise the heat to high. As soon as the broth comes to a boil, add the rice. Stir once, cover with the lid, and place the pot into the oven. Bake for 45 minutes. Remove and serve hot.

Roasted Butter Beans with Garlic 🅥

Roasting butter beans (also known as lima beans) makes them chewy and adds richness to their flavor. Tossing the frozen beans with olive oil and then straight into the oven makes this a simple weeknight vegetable option.

MAKES 4 AMPLE SERVINGS

Preheat the oven to 375°.

Spray a rimmed baking tray with nonstick cooking spray and pile the frozen beans on. Drizzle with the oil, mix them around with your hands, and then arrange the beans roughly in a single layer. Sprinkle with the salt and roast for 25 minutes.

Remove from the oven, stir in the garlic, and place back in the oven for 5 minutes longer. Remove from the oven, squeeze the lemon wedge over the top, stir, and serve warm.

2 (10-ounce) boxes frozen butter beans or baby lima beans (*not* "steam-in-the-bag" kind)

2 tablespoons olive oil

½ teaspoon kosher or sea salt

2 plump garlic cloves, microplaned or minced

1 lemon wedge

Slow Cooker Black-Eyed Peas 🌱

3 cups dried black-eyed
    peas

8 cups boiling Roasted
    Vegetable Broth (page 33)
    or Chickpea Broth
    (page 35)

1 medium yellow onion,
    chopped

1–2 teaspoons liquid smoke,
    to taste

Kosher or sea salt, to taste

Soft, smoky beans are comfort food for many. I make up a big pot of these black-eyed peas and serve steaming bowls of them (with a pat of butter on top), but I also use them as a base for so many other dishes—loaded nachos, for instance. Liquid smoke, a natural product, literally made from smoke, adds a delicious depth to the dish.

This dish is especially good served with Chow-Chow (recipe follows)—a sweet and tangy relish of sorts.

MAKES ABOUT 8 HEARTY SERVINGS

Pick through the black-eyed peas to remove any debris. Pour them into the slow cooker, then pour in the boiling broth, onions, and 1 teaspoon liquid smoke. Set the cooker on high, cover, and cook for 4 hours or until the beans are tender (the time will depend on the age of the beans—older beans take longer to soften). Season with additional liquid smoke, if you like, and salt to taste.

Chow-Chow 🥖

This pickle relish has a nice balance between sweet and tangy. It goes well with so many salty or fatty dishes, especially slow-cooked beans.

MAKES ABOUT 3 CUPS

Toss the vegetables together in a large bowl, then sprinkle in the salt and toss again. Cover loosely with plastic wrap or a clean kitchen towel and set in the fridge for 4 hours.

After 4 hours, make the dressing: Bring all the dressing ingredients to a boil in a saucepan over medium-high heat, then reduce heat to medium-low and cook, uncovered, for 2 minutes. Remove the salted vegetables from their bowl, leaving behind any expelled liquid. Add the vegetables to the dressing pan (no need to rinse them) and toss to coat the veggies with dressing. Cover and raise the heat to medium-high or high and cook for 5 minutes, stirring twice.

Store, refrigerated, in a lidded jar. Keeps for a week.

FOR THE CHOW-CHOW MIX

1 head green cabbage, core removed, leaves chopped small (about 4 cups)

¼ large red bell pepper, chopped (about ½ cup)

¼ large green bell pepper, chopped (about ½ cup)

1 small sweet onion (such as Vidalia), chopped (about 1 cup)

3 teaspoons kosher or sea salt

FOR THE DRESSING

¾ cup brown sugar, lightly packed

½ cup white vinegar

1 teaspoon mustard seeds

½ teaspoon celery seeds

½ teaspoon ground turmeric

½ teaspoon ground ginger

½ dry mustard powder

¼ teaspoon red pepper flakes

Cornbread, Sage, and "Sausage" Dressing

4 tablespoons unsalted
butter, divided

1 recipe Cornbread (page
170), cut into 1-inch
cubes (about 7–8 cups)

1 medium red onion,
chopped (about 1 cup)

2–3 celery stalks, trimmed
and chopped (about
1 cup)

1 cup corn kernels (from
2 ears fresh corn)

½ teaspoon kosher or
sea salt

¼ cup chopped fresh sage

¼ cup chopped fresh
parsley

8 ounces vegetarian
breakfast sausage
patties (such as Morning
Star Farms, Quorn, or
Gimme Lean), thawed
and crumbled

2 cups Corncob and Leek
Broth (page 32)

2 large eggs, beaten

I should have named this "triple corn dressing" because corn is used in three ways: cornbread, corn kernels, and corncob broth. Vegetarian sausage replaces pork sausage, and lots of freshly chopped herbs add more layers of flavor. Keep in mind that cornbread dressing is slightly crumbly, just like cornbread, but I think that makes the dish seem lighter.

MAKES 8 SERVINGS

Preheat the oven to 350°.

Grease a 6- to 8-quart baking dish with 1 tablespoon of the butter and set aside.

Spray a rimmed baking tray with nonstick cooking spray and lay in the cornbread cubes. Bake until just dried out, but not colored, about 10 minutes.

While the cornbread cubes are baking, sauté the onions, celery, and corn with 1 tablespoon of the butter in a sauté pan, set over medium heat, for about 5 minutes, until the onions are translucent and soft. Season with the salt.

Melt the remaining 2 tablespoons of butter.

Pour the baked cornbread cubes into a large mixing bowl, then pour the hot onions, celery, and corn, fresh herbs, and crumbled sausage over the top and gently toss to mix.

Pour the broth, melted butter, and beaten eggs over the top and mix gently. Pile the dressing into a prepared baking dish, cover with aluminum foil or a lid, and bake, covered, for 45 minutes. Serve warm.

One-Pot Pimento Mac and Cheese

4 cups Roasted Vegetable
   Broth (page 33) or
   Chickpea Broth (page 35)

3 cups pasta (broken
   spaghetti, small penne,
   or elbow macaroni
   work best)

8 ounces (1 brick) cream
   cheese, roughly cut
   into cubes

2 cups shredded sharp
   cheddar cheese

¾ cup chopped jarred
   roasted red peppers
   plus 2 tablespoons juice

Kosher or sea salt, to taste

Cayenne pepper, to taste

Y'all, this recipe blew my mind! The pasta is cooked in a skillet and never drained, then the whole dish is finished in the same pot. It. Is. So. Good!

MAKES 8 HEARTY SERVINGS

In a 10-inch cast-iron skillet or oven-safe Dutch oven, bring the broth to a boil over high heat. Stir in the pasta and reduce the heat to medium or medium-low; the broth should simmer strongly. Cook, covered, with the lid cracked, for 15 to 20 minutes, stirring often so that the pasta doesn't stick (together or to the pot). Once most of the broth is absorbed, and the pasta is al dente (not too squishy), remove from the heat and stir in the cream cheese and cheddar until they melt into a creamy-gooey sauce. Stir in the roasted peppers and juice, taste, and season with salt and cayenne, as desired. Serve hot.

Fake-on Bacon 🦃

They say that bacon is the gateway meat for vegetarians. Fatty, smoky, salty—it's so darn good that it's hard to give up. Because I couldn't find a store-bought fake bacon that was tasty enough to stand in for the real thing in a BLT sandwich, I decided to develop a recipe for it myself. Rice paper mimics bacon with its chew, crispness, and even appearance. It can be found in the international section of most grocery stores. Submerging the rice paper in the marinade allows it to soak up the smoky, salty flavors.

MAKES ABOUT 30 SLICES

Preheat the oven to 375°.

Liberally spray a baking tray with nonstick cooking spray and set aside.

Use scissors to cut the brittle rice paper into strips about the width of a piece of bacon and set the strips aside.

Whisk all the remaining ingredients together in a large, shallow bowl to make a marinade.

Take 2 rice paper strips that are roughly the same size and, holding them together, submerge them into the marinade until they are fully coated. Remove them from the marinade, allowing any excess to drip back into the bowl. Lay both coated rice strips, stuck together now, onto the prepared baking tray, and continue, 2 by 2, with the remaining strips.

Bake for 8–10 minutes, until the strips are crispy. After cooling, they will keep refrigerated in an airtight container for up to 3 days. To crisp up any limp pieces, microwave them in 15-second intervals until the pieces are as crispy as you like.

10 sheets rice paper

¼ cup low-sodium soy sauce

1 tablespoon liquid smoke

¾ teaspoon smoked paprika

½ teaspoon garlic powder (not garlic salt)

½ teaspoon onion powder (not onion salt)

2 dashes ground cumin

1 tablespoon maple syrup

1 tablespoon ketchup

2 tablespoons vegetable oil

Fried Okra

Some people only eat okra fried, and it's easy to see why. Okra has a wonderful, fresh flavor and, when fried, a delicious, crunchy crust. Pair these crunchy "lady fingers" with Mississippi Comeback Sauce (recipe follows) and you've got a solid starter or fun party food.

MAKES 4 SERVINGS

Preheat the oven to 300°.

Stir together the buttermilk and hot sauce and soak the okra halves in this mixture for 20 minutes at room temperature.

Pour the oil into a 10-inch cast-iron or other heavy skillet, cover, and set over medium heat for about 5 minutes, until the oil is hot (dip a piece of bread into oil with tongs—the oil will bubble actively when it's hot enough).

Stir together the cornstarch, flour, and cornmeal. Pull a handful of the okra halves from the buttermilk and allow them to drain slightly, then place them into the cornstarch and flour mixture and toss until evenly coated.

Carefully place the okra halves, one at a time, into the hot oil. Fry 3–5 minutes, turning once, until golden and crunchy. Season with the popcorn salt. Keep warm in the oven as the rest of the okra are fried.

1 quart buttermilk

2 tablespoons hot sauce (such as Tabasco)

1 pound fresh okra, sliced in half from stem to tip

2 cups peanut oil, for frying

1 cup cornstarch

1 cup all-purpose flour

1 cup yellow or white cornmeal

Popcorn salt

Mississippi Comeback Sauce

1 cup mayonnaise (such as
    Duke's)

1 tablespoon sambal oelek

1 teaspoon Worcestershire
    sauce

2 teaspoons ketchup

¼ teaspoon freshly ground
    black pepper

½ teaspoon dry mustard
    powder

1 teaspoon onion powder
    (not onion salt)

This sauce is so good it keeps people coming back for more. Creamy and a little spicy, it is the perfect foil for fried foods, but it's also great on a sandwich or even drizzled over grilled tofu.

Sambal oelek is a chunky, funky Indonesian garlic chili sauce that packs a good wallop of heat. You can find it in the international food section of most grocery stores. I highly recommend keeping a small jar of it in your fridge to kick up the spice factor in many dishes.

MAKES 1 HEAPING CUP

Mix all the ingredients together. Stash in the refrigerator until ready to serve—up to a week.

Sweet and Tangy Coleslaw 🅥

This noncreamy slaw is perfectly suited for "pork" barbecue; it retains most of the cabbage's crunchy appeal hours after being dressed. Even though I adore mayonnaise, I don't miss it in this recipe.

MAKES 8 SERVINGS

Whisk the sugar, vinegar, salt, and celery seeds together in a bowl until the sugar and salt are dissolved.

Toss together both of the cabbages, carrots, and green onions in a separate large bowl, then pour the dressing over and toss well to evenly coat the slaw. Cover and refrigerate for at least an hour before serving.

½ cup granulated sugar

½ cup cider vinegar

½ teaspoon kosher or
   sea salt

1 teaspoon celery seeds

½ head savoy cabbage,
   shredded

½ head red cabbage,
   shredded

1 cup grated carrots

4 green onions, chopped

Twice-Baked Not-So-Sweet Potatoes

4 medium-size sweet
    potatoes (about 4–5 cups
    when mashed)

2–3 tablespoons unsalted
    butter

1 teaspoon kosher or
    sea salt

¼ cup buttermilk

1 bunch green onions,
    chopped

2 cups shredded extra-
    sharp cheddar cheese,
    divided

I have to admit, I'm not normally a fan of sweet potatoes the way they are traditionally prepared in the South. I am missing a sweet tooth, so although I can appreciate the flavors of sweet potato casserole and the like, I'm not drawn to them.

This recipe is for anyone else out there without much of a sweet tooth. Prepared just as you would a white twice-baked potato, cooked sweet potatoes are mashed with butter, green onions, buttermilk, and sharp cheddar then stuffed back into the potato's skin and baked until the sweetness of the potato is balanced with the sharp cheese, tangy buttermilk, and herbaceous green onions—YUM!

While I developed this recipe using easily found orange sweet potatoes, I've also made it with purple yams, which are absolutely gorgeous and even less sweet than their orange cousins.

MAKES 8

Pierce each sweet potato several times with the tip of a sharp knife.

Microwave them altogether in a microwave-safe dish for 10–15 minutes; check after 10 minutes to see if all the potatoes are soft, if some aren't, remove the ones that are, turn the others over, and keep cooking.

Once all the potatoes are done, carefully slice each in half lengthwise (use a kitchen towel to handle them—they'll be hot) and scoop the cooked flesh into a large bowl.

Preheat the oven to 375°, if you'll be serving the potatoes immediately.

Use a potato masher or a sturdy fork to mash the butter and salt into the hot potatoes, then add the buttermilk and continue mashing. If you desire lump-free potatoes, pass the cooked potatoes through a ricer, then add the butter, buttermilk, and salt.

Once the mash is mixed and cooled, stir in the green onions and half of the cheddar. Fill each half with the mash. Place them on a rimmed baking tray sprayed with nonstick cooking spray and top each of the filled potatoes evenly with the remaining cheddar.

Bake 20–30 minutes, until the cheese is melted and bubbly.

These can easily be made ahead up to where they are topped with cheese, then held in the fridge for up to a day before baking, but they will need to bake a bit longer because they are starting out cold.

Memphis Mustard Slaw 🖐

1 head green cabbage,
    sliced very thin, avoiding
    the core
2 large carrots, peeled and
    sliced thinly or shredded
1 green bell pepper, diced
1 large jalapeño pepper,
    minced (for extra heat,
    use the seeds and
    membrane, otherwise
    discard)
½ cup granulated sugar
½ teaspoon kosher or
    sea salt
¼ cup cider vinegar
½ cup yellow mustard
¾ cup vegan mayonnaise
½ small red onion,
    microplaned or
    shredded, with juice

This is a unique twist on classic creamy coleslaw. Yellow mustard plays an important factor in flavoring this slaw and giving it a beautiful color. Serve it as you would classic coleslaw.

Make sure to slice the cabbage, rather than shredding it in a box grater or food processor; it stays crisp longer.

MAKES 8 SERVINGS

Toss the cabbage, carrots, bell peppers, and jalapeños together in a large bowl.

Make the dressing: Whisk the sugar, salt, and vinegar together until the sugar and salt are dissolved. Whisk in all the rest of the ingredients until smooth, then pour over the cabbage mixture and toss to coat evenly. Refrigerate for at least an hour and up to a day before serving.

Rutmus

When we lived in northwest England we often traveled farther north still to Scotland. All six of us, even our twins, who were just toddlers, fell in love with the lush Scottish countryside and the beautiful city of Edinburgh.

And the food—oh my Lord, Scottish food is fabulous, aside from their beloved fried Mars Bars. Neeps and tatties quickly became a favorite of our whole family. It's often served with haggis (animal stomach stuffed with other critter organs, oats, and spices, then boiled—honestly, I swear, it's delicious), but neeps and tatties is a marvelous vegetarian dish. Mashed potatoes receive a flavor kick with the simple addition of turnips.

Rutmus is the southern version of neeps and tatties. We make it with rutabaga rather than turnips. Both vegetables are brassicas, but turnips are smaller with a white interior, while rutabagas are larger and have a yellow flesh.

This dish tastes very similar to mashed potatoes, just slightly more complex. Make sure to follow the timing of cooking the vegetables—their different densities require different cooking times.

MAKES 6 SERVINGS

1½ pounds rutabaga, skin trimmed off, cut into ½-inch cubes (about 4 cups)

1½ pounds baking potatoes, skin peeled off, cut into 1½-inch cubes (about 4 cups)

1 teaspoon kosher or sea salt

8 tablespoons (1 stick) butter, cubed, divided

Bring a large pot of water to a boil, then add the rutabaga cubes, cover with the lid cracked, return to a simmer, and cook for 5 minutes.

After 5 minutes, add the potato cubes, cover with the lid cracked, return to a simmer, and cook for 10 minutes longer.

Test a rutabaga cube to make sure it's tender; if so, drain very well, then pour the cooked rutabaga and potatoes back into the cooking pot and use a potato masher or ricer to mash the vegetables with the salt and 6 tablespoons of the butter cubes.

Once the Rutmus is the consistency you like, place the remaining butter cubes on top, cover, and allow the butter to melt. Serve hot.

Wilmer's Potato Salad

3 pounds red potatoes,
     cubed
1 tablespoon kosher or
     sea salt, plus more
     for seasoning
2 heaping tablespoons
     Dijon mustard
¼ cup sour cream
½ cup mayonnaise
1 cup finely minced celery
½ cup finely chopped
     fresh chives
Freshly ground black
     pepper, to taste

At eighty-four years old, my mother still has eyes as inquisitive and expressive as in the pictures of her as a child. When she's talking about food, her face lights up and her eyes sparkle with energy and interest.

She looked like that the day she was telling me about Wilmer's potato salad. In the late 1930s, my mother would often have play-dates with her friend Susan. On the days that Susan's dad, Wilmer, made potato salad for dinner, my mother would request that they play at Susan's house, where they'd help themselves to bowls of the ice-cold potato salad as a snack. It's nearly eighty years later and my mother is still talking about that potato salad.

She told me that Wilmer's secret was to stir the just-boiled, hot potatoes with mustard, then allow them to cool to room temperature before mixing in the dressing.

It's the best potato salad I've ever had. I always keep a bowl of it in the fridge for my children to have as an after-school snack.

MAKES 6 SERVINGS

Fill a large soup pot three-quarters full with very hot water, add the salt, cover, and bring to a boil. Carefully pour the cubed potatoes into the boiling water and cover. Return to a boil and cook for 5–10 minutes, until the potato cubes are just barely tender and easily pierced with the tip of a sharp knife.

Drain immediately in a colander, then pile the cooked potato cubes into a large bowl and toss with the mustard. Stir every 10 minutes or so until the potatoes have cooled to room temperature.

Whisk together the sour cream and mayonnaise until smooth, then stir in the celery and chives and spoon over the cooled potatoes; toss to coat evenly. Season with the black pepper, cover, and chill. Season with salt to taste once the potato salad is well chilled.

Spicy Tomato Aspic 🅥

My mother's mother, Jeanette, was known for her sense of humor, sense of style, and positive attitude, but not so much for her cooking skills (as a result, she and my grandfather ate out a lot). On special occasions, she made tomato aspic with green olives and canned crabmeat (the inexpensive kind found in the canned fish aisle). Maybe it was because she rarely cooked or because she was so beloved, but when she made her tomato aspic, the whole family got excited—to this day, my siblings, cousins, aunts, uncles, and I adore that dish. It's a very genteel, old-school southern dish that is fabulous in the summer for lunch.

I've taken her original recipe, gotten rid of the crabmeat, and spiced it up significantly using Tabasco green olives. If you don't care for heat, use regular green olives.

MAKES 8 SLICES

5 cups tomato juice, divided
4 packets unflavored gelatin
3 tablespoons fresh lemon juice
½ cup chopped Tabasco or regular green olives
½ cup finely chopped celery
1 teaspoon kosher or sea salt
1 teaspoon Worcestershire sauce
½ teaspoon hot sauce (such as Tabasco)
Fresh green herbs or lettuce leaves, for garnish

Spray a 6-cup mold or loaf pan with nonstick cooking spray and set aside.

Bring 3 cups of the tomato juice to a strong simmer. Stir all 4 packets of the gelatin into the remaining 2 cups of tomato juice and allow it to sit for 1 minute. Pour the hot tomato juice into the gelatin and tomato juice, add the remaining ingredients, and stir to distribute evenly. Pour into the prepared mold and refrigerate overnight.

Unmold the aspic onto a serving platter and garnish with the herbs or lettuce. If the aspic sticks to the mold, gently hold the mold under very hot running water, being careful not to get any water into the aspic, for 1–2 seconds, and it should slip out easily.

Potlikker Greens 🌱

2 medium yellow onions, sliced (about 4 cups)

2 tablespoons vegetable oil

10 large collard greens, stem cut out and discarded, leaves chopped (about 10 cups)

½ teaspoon kosher or sea salt

3 cups Chickpea Broth (page 35)

2 tablespoons cider vinegar

Hot sauce (such as Tabasco), for serving

Potlikker is the flavorful liquid left in the pot after cooking greens. It's a great base for soups or just sopped up with a biscuit or hoecake. Classically, the likker is seasoned not only by juices released from the greens but by a smoked ham hock that's been bobbing around as the greens cook for hours. I figured out a way to replace the ham hock with the equally good flavor of caramelized onions. The onions add depth and sweetness to the greens that aren't typical, but fabulous in their own right.

MAKES 4–6 SERVINGS

Set a large, heavy pot over medium-high heat and sauté the onions in the oil for 5 minutes, until they just start to color. Reduce the heat to medium-low and continue to sauté, very gently, as the onions color and caramelize, about 15 minutes longer; if the pot gets dry, splash in ½ cup water and continue cooking.

Place the collards into the pot along with the salt and broth. Stir, cover, and raise the temperature to medium. Bring to a simmer and simmer for 15 minutes.

Add the vinegar and taste to check if it needs more salt. Serve with hot sauce.

Hushpuppies

I have a friend named Ansle who grew up in Charlotte, North Carolina. She has seen her home grow and change from a largely agrarian region to the country's second largest banking center. Little of the area is the same as when she was a child.

Ansle popped over to pick up her daughter from our house on the day I was developing this hushpuppy recipe. As with every person who enters my home, I asked Ansle if she would taste what I was cooking. She crunched into one and said, "These are just like we used to eat at the fish camps when I was little! We would eat pounds of these along with fried fish." In that moment, the flavors were exactly as they were when she was a child in Charlotte, as if nothing had changed.

MAKES ABOUT 2 DOZEN 2-INCH HUSHPUPPIES

Pour the vegetable oil into a 10-inch cast-iron or other heavy skillet and set over medium heat.

Stir together the flour, cornmeal, salt, sugar, and baking soda. In a separate bowl, whisk together the buttermilk and egg. Use a microplane or the small holes of a box grater to grate 2 tablespoons of onion purée and juice from the onion and stir that into the buttermilk and egg mixture. Stir the wet ingredients into the dry until just combined and there are no lumps.

Once the oil is shimmering, use either a small portion scoop (such as a small ice cream scoop) or a teaspoon to take scoops of the batter and drop them carefully into the hot oil. Make sure they don't stick to the bottom of the skillet as they cook. Fry, turning once so that both sides become golden, 3–5 minutes in total. You should have about 24 (2-inch) hushpuppies. Drain on a wire rack or paper towels and season with popcorn salt.

1–2 cups vegetable oil, for frying
1 cup all-purpose flour
1 cup yellow or white cornmeal
1 teaspoon kosher or sea salt
1½ teaspoons granulated sugar
¾ teaspoon baking soda
¾ cup buttermilk
1 large egg
½ small yellow onion
Popcorn salt

Truffle and Mushroom Grits

FOR THE GRITS

FOR THE GRITS

1 large shallot, minced
   (about ⅔ cup)

2 plump garlic cloves,
   microplaned or minced

2 tablespoons unsalted
   butter

8 ounces shiitake
   mushrooms, stems
   discarded, caps sliced

8 ounces cremini
   mushrooms, stems
   discarded, caps sliced

8 ounces oyster
   mushrooms, chopped

¼ teaspoon kosher or
   sea salt

4 cups Umami Mushroom
   Broth (page 38)

1 cup stone-ground yellow
   or white grits

FOR THE SAUCE

1 tablespoon unsalted
   butter

1½ tablespoons all-purpose
   flour

1 cup half-and-half

½ cup grated Parmigiano-
   Reggiano cheese

¼ teaspoon truffle salt

1 teaspoon truffle oil

Truffle anything makes me weak in the knees. Truffle fries, scrambled eggs, risotto, pasta, cheese—if it says "truffle" on the menu, I'm ordering it.

But unless you are eating at an extremely expensive restaurant, the truffle flavor you taste is most likely synthetic. Real truffles and synthetic truffle flavor taste very different from each other, but you know what? I love them both! There's room for each, in abundance, on my dinner table.

Fresh truffles have an exceptionally delicate shelf life: once dug up they should be consumed within days. They also have an insane price tag, running up to $3,600 per pound, which makes them out of reach for most people. Truffle oil and truffle salt are the way most people get that truffle flavor blast onto their palates.

This recipe uses both truffle salt and oil in the white truffle sauce, paired with three types of mushrooms and flavorful Umami Mushroom Broth.

MAKES 4 HEARTY SERVINGS

To make the grits, place a large saucepan over medium-high heat and sauté the shallots and garlic in butter until the shallots are translucent, about 2–3 minutes. Add the mushrooms to the pan, season with the salt, stir, reduce the heat to medium, and cover. Cook, covered, for about 5 minutes.

As soon as the mushrooms release their yummy juices, pour in the broth, raise the heat to medium-high, and cover with the lid cracked. Bring the broth to a boil. Add the grits in a steady stream, whisking or stirring with a wooden spoon constantly as you go. Lower the heat to medium-low or low and keep whisking or stirring for 2 minutes (this will help prevent lumps). Continue cooking, uncovered, stirring every few minutes, until the grits are thick, soft, and creamy, about 35 minutes. A few bubbles should regularly break at the top of the grits, but the grits should not be simmering.

To make the sauce, melt the butter in a small saucepan set over medium heat. Add the flour and stir to combine: you are making a roux (a thickening agent). Cook for 1 minute, then pour in the half-and-half and whisk; it will thicken as it comes to a simmer— do not let it boil. Once the sauce reaches a simmer, stir and allow it to gently bubble away for 1 minute, then turn off the heat and stir in the Parmigiano-Reggiano, truffle salt, and truffle oil.

To serve, scoop the grits onto plates or bowls and generously drizzle the top with truffle sauce.

Sweet Breakfast Grits

4 cups whole milk

¼ cup light brown sugar, packed

¼ teaspoon ground cinnamon

Dash of ground nutmeg

½ teaspoon vanilla extract

1 cup stone-ground yellow or white grits

There is something so nice about a warm breakfast. A bowlful of something sweet and creamy beckoning from the breakfast table is indeed a treat, but not possible for many of us with rushed morning routines. This is a perfect recipe to make on the weekend, when life moves somewhat more slowly and we sleep in just a bit.

MAKES 4 HEARTY SERVINGS

Bring all the ingredients except the grits to a simmer in a medium saucepan over medium heat. Add the grits in a steady stream, whisking or stirring with a wooden spoon constantly as you go. Lower the heat to medium-low or low and keep whisking or stirring for 2 minutes (this will help prevent lumps). Continue cooking, uncovered, stirring every few minutes, until the grits are thick, soft, and creamy, about 35 minutes. A few bubbles should regularly break at the top of the grits, but the grits should not be simmering. Serve with butter and maple syrup or, better yet, a dollop of Overnight Apple Butter (recipe follows).

Overflight Apple Butter 🍏

4–5 pounds baking apples,
such as Granny Smith,
cored, skin left on, cut
into 1-inch cubes
¾ cup light brown sugar,
packed
¼ cup granulated sugar
½ teaspoon kosher or
sea salt
2 teaspoons vanilla extract
1 teaspoon ground
cinnamon
⅛ teaspoon ground nutmeg
1 tablespoon cider vinegar

One of my earliest food memories is of apple butter. We lived near a wonderful open-air produce market called Tuller's. In the fall they carried all types of apples, but they also fried doughnuts, made apple pies, and sold jars of apple butter.

I love apple butter because it's not too sweet and is silky smooth—perfect for spreading on buttered toast in the morning.

Making apple butter in the slow cooker is so easy it's almost embarrassing; it tastes as if you've spent hours tending to it when really it's been cooking while you slept. In the morning, your house will smell like an apple pie.

MAKES ABOUT 4 CUPS

Spray a 5- or 6-quart slow cooker with nonstick cooking spray. Toss the apple cubes with both the sugars, salt, vanilla, cinnamon, nutmeg, and vinegar, then pile everything into the slow cooker.

Cover and turn the setting to low. Cook at least 8 hours or overnight.

Purée with an immersion blender or transfer to a stand blender to purée. If it's slightly watery, pour the apple butter back into the slow cooker, turn the setting to high, and cook, uncovered, for an hour. The apple butter will also thicken as it cools.

Store in clean jars in the fridge for up to a week.

Carolina Grits with Sweet Potato Swirl and Smoked Gouda

This is as pretty a dish as it is tasty. Cheesy grits are swirled with sweet potato purée, then dotted with spicy Sriracha and topped with vibrant green onions.

MAKES 4 SERVINGS

Prick the sweet potato several times all over with a fork or the tip of a sharp knife. Place the potato on a plate and microwave for 5–8 minutes, until very soft all the way through. Allow it to cool, then scrape the flesh from the skin (discard the skin) and use a fork or potato masher to mash it with the milk, salt, and honey until very smooth. Set aside.

In a large saucepan bring the milk, water, and salt to a simmer over medium-high heat. Add the grits in a steady stream, whisking or stirring with a wooden spoon constantly as you go. Lower the heat to medium-low or low and keep whisking or stirring for 2 minutes (this will help prevent lumps). Continue cooking, uncovered, stirring every few minutes, until the grits are thick, soft, and creamy, about 35 minutes. A few bubbles should regularly break at the top of the grits, but the grits should not be simmering. Once the grits are cooked, remove from the heat and stir in the butter and Gouda. Cover for up to (but no longer than) 5 minutes before serving.

Spoon the sweet potato purée into a zip-top sandwich bag and snip off one corner. Spoon the grits onto plates or into bowls and gently squeeze the sweet potato purée in concentric circles on top of the grits. If you are using the sriracha, dot it around the circles, and then scatter the green onions over the top.

FOR THE SWEET POTATO PURÉE

1 1-pound sweet potato

1½ cups whole milk

¼ teaspoon kosher or sea salt

2 teaspoons honey

FOR THE GRITS

2 cups whole milk

2 cups water

1 teaspoon kosher or sea salt

1 cup stone-ground yellow or white grits

2 tablespoons unsalted butter, cubed

4 ounces smoked Gouda cheese, shredded

Sriracha (optional, for heat)

4 green onions, chopped

Fried Green Tomatoes

3 medium green tomatoes

Kosher or sea salt

Vegetable oil, for frying

1 teaspoon onion powder (not onion salt)

½ teaspoon garlic powder (not garlic salt)

¼ cup all-purpose flour

¼ cup cornstarch

½ cup buttermilk

1 large egg

¾ cup yellow or white cornmeal

¾ cup breadcrumbs

Fried green tomatoes are a summertime treat. I like to fry green tomatoes that have just started to ripen, getting streaks of yellow, at which point they aren't so tart. Fried up, they have a crisp, delicate crust that yields to a beautifully soft interior. Pimento Aioli is a wonderful accompaniment to these either as is or in a sandwich.

MAKES 6 SERVINGS

Trim the stems off the tomatoes and slice each tomato into ½-inch slices. Season the tomato slices lightly with salt and set them on a dinner plate lined with paper towels for 10–20 minutes to draw out liquid; this makes the tomatoes fry up crispy.

Pour ¼ inch of oil into a cast-iron or other heavy skillet. Cover and turn the heat on to just slightly below medium, allowing the oil to heat for about 5 minutes.

Evenly season both sides of the tomato slices with the onion and garlic powders. Stir the flour and cornstarch together in a bowl. In a separate bowl, whisk together the buttermilk and egg, and in a third bowl, stir together the cornmeal and breadcrumbs.

Coat a few of the tomato slices with the flour and cornstarch mixture, then dip into the buttermilk and egg mixture, and finally coat in the cornmeal and breadcrumbs—bread only the slices that are about to go into the oil. Place the breaded slices into the hot oil, being careful not to crowd the skillet. The oil should be bubbling consistently around each tomato slice.

Fry until the first side is golden, 4–5 minutes, then turn over and fry the other side until golden, 4 minutes longer. Drain on a wire rack or paper towels. Serve immediately with Pimento Aioli (recipe follows).

Pimento Aioli

This tasty, garlicky sauce is great on fried green tomatoes, on "crab" cakes, or in place of mayonnaise on sandwiches. It's a snap to whip up and keeps for a week in the fridge.

MAKES 1 CUP

Stir everything together and store in the refrigerator.

1 cup mayonnaise (such as Duke's)

¼ cup finely chopped jarred roasted red peppers plus 2 teaspoons juice

2 plump garlic cloves, microplaned or minced

Stuffed Yellow Summer Squash

3 medium yellow squash

¼ cup olive oil, divided

Kosher or sea salt, to taste

1 plump garlic clove, microplaned or minced

½ small yellow onion, chopped (about ½ cup)

1½ cups cooked and cooled quinoa

2–3 ounces feta cheese, crumbled

1 heaping tablespoon chopped, fresh dill weed

½ cup chopped fresh parsley

2 teaspoons fresh lemon juice

1 tablespoon extra-virgin olive oil

This is a great dish to make in the summer not only because of the abundance of yellow squash but also because it can be made ahead and served cold, like a salad—great to eat al fresco!

MAKES 6

Preheat the oven to 375°.

Slice the squash in half lengthwise from stem to tip. Score each half: cut crisscross lines into the squash halves without cutting all the way through. Scoop out the flesh, leaving the skin intact. Chop the flesh into fine pieces and set aside.

Rub a little oil into each hollowed-out squash half, then season with salt and roast in the oven, cut-side down, for 15–20 minutes, until the squash is just soft but not collapsed.

Sauté the garlic, onions, and squash in 1 tablespoon of the olive oil for 10 minutes in a skillet set over medium-high heat and season with salt. If the squash begins to stick, add 1 tablespoon of either oil or water to the skillet.

Pour the cooked vegetables into a large bowl, then stir in the quinoa, crumbled feta, dill, and parsley. Whisk together the lemon juice and olive oil, then drizzle over the mixture and stir.

Fill each of the squash halves with the quinoa mixture and serve or chill, covered, in the fridge for up to 4 hours.

Pickles

Pickles play an important role on the southern table.
We pickle far more than just cucumbers down here.
Beets, onions, and Jerusalem artichokes—all add a
sweet tang to a formal dinner, slathered on sandwiches,
or complementing salty cheeses or casseroles.

Pickled Okra 🄷

Okra were made to be pickled. Because the pods are naturally fibrous, they develop a crisp crunch after a good soak in the tart brine. The sugar in this doesn't make the pickles overtly sweet—it just balances them out nicely with the salt. If you are sensitive to the slime factor of okra, pickling the pods whole (not sliced into halves) will cut down considerably on the goo.

You can pack the pickled okra in large or small jars—the end result is the same.

MAKES SLIGHTLY MORE THAN 1 QUART

Place the brine ingredients into a small saucepan and bring to a simmer, covered, over medium-high heat. Once the brine comes to a simmer, reduce the heat to medium-low and gently cook, covered, for 10 minutes.

Arrange the okra, chili peppers, garlic, ginger, and onion in clean jars and carefully pour the simmering brine over top. The brine needs to cover the okra by ½ inch. Screw the lids on and allow the hot jars to cool to room temperature, then place them in the fridge. Keep refrigerated for up to 3 weeks.

FOR THE BRINE

3 cups cider vinegar

3 cups water

12 dried allspice berries

12 black peppercorns

1 tablespoon mustard seeds

2 bay leaves

1 cup granulated sugar

⅓ cup kosher or sea salt

FOR THE OKRA

1½ pounds fresh okra, sliced in half from stem to tip

2 red hot chili peppers, sliced in half from stem to tip

2 plump garlic cloves, smashed

1-inch fresh ginger root, sliced (no need to peel)

½ medium red onion, sliced (about 2 cups)

Dill Pickled Beets 🔵

2 bunches fresh beets,
    greens trimmed off,
    skins remaining
½ cup white sugar
2 teaspoons kosher or
    sea salt
½ cup water
1 cup white or cider vinegar
1 teaspoon dill seeds
1 small yellow onion, sliced
Handful of fresh dill weed,
    on stems

People who proclaim not to like beets are always surprised that they love these. I adore beets, especially when cold and pickled. This recipe is well balanced, not too acidic, not too sweet, and with a nice dill flavor, but not overwhelmingly so. The beets are great as a side dish, on salads, or eaten as a snack, as I do often. I always have a jar in the fridge for munching.

MAKES 1 QUART

Preheat the oven to 400°.

Either wrap the whole beets together tightly in aluminum foil or place in a lidded cast-iron skillet (rubbed with a bit of oil). Roast the beets for 45 minutes, remove from the oven, unwrap or uncover, and allow to cool until they can be easily handled. Slip off the skins and slice each beet into ¼-inch rounds, then slice the rounds into half moons.

Place the sugar, salt, water, and vinegar into a small saucepan and set over medium heat. Cook until the sugar and salt have dissolved, then add the dill seeds and cook for 1 minute longer. Remove from the heat.

Take a clean, 1-quart canning jar and alternate laying the beet and the onion slices; tuck the fresh dill weed in there, too. Carefully pour the dill brine into the filled jar covering the beets by ½ inch. Place the lid on the jar and allow to cool at room temperature, then store in the fridge for up to 3 weeks.

Easy Artichoke Relish 🐷

1 pound Jerusalem
    artichokes, also called
    sunchokes

1 cup light brown sugar,
    lightly packed

1½ cups cider vinegar

1 teaspoon mustard seeds

½ teaspoon celery seeds

1 teaspoon ground turmeric

1 teaspoon kosher or
    sea salt

1 bird's eye chili pepper or
    ¼ teaspoon red pepper
    flakes

1 tablespoon pickling spice,
    tied in cheesecloth

½ large red bell pepper,
    trimmed, seeded and
    diced small

1 small yellow onion, diced
    small

2 tablespoons cornstarch

I'd never heard of artichoke relish until we moved to Augusta, Georgia, where I was food writer for the *Augusta Chronicle*. I wrote a story about how generations of families would gather in the fall to can artichoke relish together. It was and remains a wonderful example of food and cooking bridging generation gaps, keeping families close. I also learned that, interestingly, artichoke relish doesn't contain artichokes. It uses tubers called Jerusalem artichokes, also known as sunchokes, whose flavor is similar to artichokes.

As much as I loved artichoke relish, with its vibrant yellow color, tangy flavor, and crunchy texture, I never made it at home—the canning process intimidated me. So it wasn't until I sat down to write this book that I figured out how to overcome the canning obstacle. The recipe is the same as for canning, but it stops short of processing. Just make sure to keep the relish in your fridge, and it will last up to three weeks.

MAKES ABOUT 1 QUART

Do not skin the Jerusalem artichokes. Simply chop them into very small pieces and set aside.

Combine the sugar, vinegar, mustard seeds, celery seeds, turmeric, salt, chili pepper (or red pepper flakes), and pickling spice in a medium saucepan and set over medium heat. Bring to a gentle simmer, cover with the lid cracked, and cook for 10 minutes.

Toss the Jerusalem artichokes, bell peppers, and onions with the cornstarch. Remove the pickling spice from the brine, then toss the vegetables into the simmering vinegar. Bring back to a gentle simmer and cook, uncovered, for 10–15 minutes, stirring regularly. Taste an artichoke piece at 10 minutes and decide if you like the crunch (stop cooking) or want it a bit softer (cook for 5 minutes longer).

Pour the relish into a clean 1-quart jar (you may have a bit left over), screw on the lid, and allow to cool completely at room temperature, then store in the fridge for up to 3 weeks. Excellent served on a cheese board.

Tickled Pink Onions 🌶️

There is a jar of these pink pickled onions in our refrigerator at all times. When we lived in England, I discovered a simply sublime sandwich that quickly became my favorite: cheese and onion. Take two thick pieces of fresh bakery bread and smear them with butter, then lay in slices of sharp cheddar and a bunch of these pickled onions. It is a crunchy, tangy, creamy treat!

MAKES ABOUT 3 CUPS

Lay the onion slices into a 1-quart glass jar (with lid).

Stir the boiling water together with the cloves, vinegar, sugar, and salt until the sugar and salt are dissolved. Pour the hot brine into the jar, covering the onions completely by ½ inch, screw the lid on tightly, and allow the jar to cool to room temperature before storing in the fridge for up to 3 weeks.

2 medium red onions, cut in half root to tip, peeled, then sliced into thin half moons (about 3 cups)

1 cup boiling water

10 whole cloves

1 cup white wine vinegar

¼ cup granulated sugar

1 tablespoon kosher or sea salt

Salted Carrot Coins 🥕

9 large carrots, peeled and
    cut into rounds or coins
    (about 3 cups)
1 tablespoon kosher or
    sea salt
2 tablespoons granulated
    sugar
3 tablespoons rice wine
    vinegar
1 teaspoon dried dill weed

My friend Fusako grew up in Kyoto, Japan. We became friends when our daughters were in the same preschool class in Zurich, Switzerland. Fusako is immeasurably generous with her time and attention. She would host luncheons for all the preschool moms, spending hours preparing the most beautiful Japanese dishes. Fusako's mother was equally kind. When she visited Switzerland from Kyoto, she made little dolls by hand for my four daughters; we still cherish them today.

Fusako taught me about *tsukemono*, Japanese pickles, made by salting and pressing vegetables as a means of pickling them.

I've taken inspiration from *tsukemono* to make these lovely little carrot coin pickles. Salting infuses the carrots with flavor and softens them a bit, but they still retain a good crunch. Sugar adds balance, and the vinegar gives a delicate tartness.

MAKES 3 CUPS

Toss the carrot coins with the salt and sugar in a gallon-size zip-top bag. Lay the bag on a flat surface, spreading the carrots evenly within the bag, then place a baking tray on top of the bag and pile a few heavy pots, books, or 28-ounce cans on top of the baking tray.

After an hour, pour the carrots into a colander and rinse with water; rinse out and dry the bag as well. Place the carrot coins back into the bag (or into a clean jar) and pour the vinegar and dill weed over the carrots. The carrot coins will be well seasoned and delicious within a few hours, even better the next day, and good refrigerated for up to a week.

Breads from the Oven, Skillet, and Slow Cooker

Biscuits are a given in a southern cookbook but can be an intimidating endeavor for some cooks. Drop biscuits are a fantastic way to enter into the world of home biscuit-baking—they're super easy. The Cheddar and Herb Biscuits are in an entirely different category of comfort and flavor. If you've never made hoecakes, try these—they're as easy to make as pancakes but have a wonderful corn flavor and crunch.

Cheddar and Herb Biscuits

4 ounces sharp cheddar
cheese

1 stick butter, plus
1 tablespoon for greasing
the pan

2 cups all-purpose flour

1 tablespoon baking powder

¾ teaspoon kosher or
sea salt

⅓ cup finely chopped
fresh chives

1 cup buttermilk (not
low-fat), very cold

1 plump garlic clove,
microplaned or minced

2 tablespoons unsalted
butter, melted

Friends and family have been rendered speechless by these biscuits. Eaten hot, right out of the oven (as all biscuits should be), their bottoms are crispy, their interiors are light, fluffy, and moist, and there are tiny pools of melted cheddar hiding within. They are sublime and a little dangerous—it is impossible to eat just one.

MAKES 20

Cut the cheese into ¼-inch cubes. Do not skip this step or use shredded cheese—these little cubes create the cheese pools within the baked biscuits. Lay the cheese cubes in a single layer on a piece of parchment paper or on a plate. Place the cheese and the stick of butter in the freezer and freeze for 30 minutes.

Preheat the oven to 425°.

Grease a baking sheet with the tablespoon of butter.

Sir together the flour, baking powder, salt, and chives until evenly combined. Grate the frozen butter stick (using a box grater) directly into the flour, scattering in the frozen cheese cubes in as well. Stir quickly to incorporate, then stir in the buttermilk. Mix only until a shaggy dough develops.

Use a small portion scoop (such as a small ice cream scoop) or a tablespoon to scoop the biscuits, placing them on the buttered baking sheet. You should have about 20 (2-inch) biscuits. Place them close together, their sides barely touching, for soft-sided biscuits, or separated for crispy-sided biscuits.

Bake immediately in the preheated oven for 15–30 minutes, depending on size. They are done when they're risen and golden. While they are baking, stir the garlic into the melted butter. Brush the biscuits just out of the oven with the garlic butter and serve immediately.

Slow Cooker Pecan Cinnamon Rolls with Buttermilk–Cream Cheese Glaze

FOR THE DOUGH

1¼ cup whole milk

1 tablespoon active dry yeast

¼ cup granulated sugar, divided

4–4¼ cups all-purpose flour

1 teaspoon kosher or sea salt

FOR THE FILLING

5 tablespoons unsalted butter, softened

1 tablespoon ground cinnamon

½ cup granulated sugar

¼ cup light brown sugar, packed

½ teaspoon vanilla extract

Pinch of kosher or sea salt

½ cup pecan pieces

FOR THE GLAZE

4 ounces (½ block) cream cheese

½ cup powdered sugar

2 tablespoons buttermilk

1 teaspoon vanilla extract

I don't have a sweet tooth, and maybe because of that I don't often think about baking, but these cinnamon rolls are the exception. "Baking" them in a slow cooker means that there is no need to proof the dough, the oven won't heat up the kitchen, and they are done in as little as 90 minutes. The rolls alone are not overtly sweet, but with the addition of the simple buttermilk cream cheese glaze, they hit the sweet mark. If you don't care for nuts, simply leave them out; it won't affect the recipe.

MAKES 12

Warm the milk in the microwave or on the stove until just warm to the touch. Pour the yeast into the warm milk, add 1 teaspoon of the sugar, and stir once, cover with a plate or plastic wrap, and allow the yeast to bloom and become frothy, about 5 minutes.

While the yeast is blooming, make the filling: Stir together all the filling ingredients except the pecans. Set aside.

Fit a stand mixer with a dough paddle and pour 4 cups of the flour, remaining sugar, and salt into the work bowl. Mix briefly to distribute everything evenly, then pour in the frothy yeast milk, scraping the bowl to get out all of the yeast. Mix on low for 1 minute, then on medium-low for 2 minutes longer. Stop the mixer and scrape down the sides and bottom to make sure all the flour is being incorporated; mix again for 1–2 minutes, until the dough pulls away from the bowl. If it seems too wet and isn't pulling away from the bowl, add the remaining flour, 1 tablespoon at a time, until the dough pulls away from the bowl.

Remove the dough to a lightly floured surface and knead for 5 minutes, then place back into the mixing bowl, cover with a dishtowel, and set in a nondrafty place (a microwave, turned off, works great for this).

Allow the dough to rest for 5–10 minutes, then, on a lightly floured surface, roll the dough out to about a 20 × 10-inch rectangle. Spread the filling evenly over the rectangle, leaving a 1-inch border around the 2 longest sides and sprinkle with the pecans.

Roll up evenly into a log, then trim off any ragged ends and cut the log into 2-inch rounds.

Spray a 5- or 6-quart slow cooker with nonstick cooking spray and insert a large piece of parchment paper that comes up the sides. Snuggle the cinnamon roll rounds into the prepared cooker, cinnamon swirl–side up, then lay 2 paper towels on top of the cooker, not touching the rolls; place the lid on, and turn the setting to high. The paper towels will absorb the condensation that may otherwise make the rolls soggy.

"Bake" the cinnamon rolls for 90 minutes, then check for doneness by inserting a sharp knife into the middle—if it comes out clean, the rolls are done, if it's sticky, they need more time, up to 30 minutes longer.

Make the glaze: Warm the cream cheese in a microwave until just barely soft, then stir in the powdered sugar, buttermilk, and vanilla.

When the rolls are ready, pull them out of the slow cooker using the parchment paper. Lay on a platter and drizzle with the buttermilk–cream cheese glaze. Serve warm.

Easy Drop Biscuits

2 cups all-purpose flour

1 tablespoon baking powder

¾ teaspoon kosher or
   sea salt

1 stick butter, frozen
   30 minutes

1 cup buttermilk (not low-
   fat), very cold

These are the best biscuits for a novice baker to attempt or anyone wanting biscuits, fast. No rolling, no kneading—just scoop onto a greased baking sheet.

I like making them small, but the recipe works well for larger biscuits, too; simply adjust the baking time.

MAKES ABOUT 20

Preheat the oven to 425°.

Grease a baking sheet with 1 tablespoon of butter.

Sir together the flour, baking powder, and salt until evenly combined. Grate the frozen butter stick (using a box grater) directly into the flour, stir quickly to incorporate, then stir in the buttermilk. Mix only until a shaggy dough develops.

Use a small portion scoop (such as a small ice cream scoop) or a tablespoon to scoop the biscuits, placing them on the buttered baking sheet. You should have about 20 (2-inch) biscuits. Place them close together, their sides barely touching, for soft-sided biscuits or separated for crispy-sided biscuits.

Bake immediately in the preheated oven for 15–30 minutes, depending on size. They are done when they're risen and golden.

Hoecakes

Hoecakes are crunchy little cornmeal pancakes. They are great for sopping up gravy or potlikker and wonderful when eaten as George Washington did, drizzled with honey. Because their flavor lies somewhere between sweet and savory, they make a fine accompaniment at breakfast, lunch, or dinner.

MAKES ABOUT 12 (3-INCH) CAKES

Set a cast-iron or other heavy skillet over medium heat.

Mix the flour, cornmeal, baking powder, salt, and sugar together. Whisk in the eggs, buttermilk, and melted butter until there are no lumps.

Lightly coat the bottom of the pan with oil. Pour in roughly 2 tablespoons of the batter into the hot pan—it should sizzle when it hits the oil; cook until golden on one side and little air holes open up on the edges of the cake (the same as with pancakes), about 2 minutes. Flip the hoecakes over and cook the other side until crisp and golden, another 2 minutes.

1 cup self-rising flour

1 cup yellow or white cornmeal

1 teaspoon baking powder

1 teaspoon kosher or sea salt

2 teaspoons granulated sugar

2 large eggs

1 cup buttermilk

2 tablespoons unsalted butter, melted

Vegetable oil, for sautéing

Cornbread

8 tablespoons (1 stick
butter), divided

½ cup plus 2 tablespoons
all-purpose flour

1¾ cups yellow or white
cornmeal

1 tablespoon plus
1 teaspoon granulated
sugar

1¼ teaspoons kosher or
sea salt

1 tablespoon plus
1 teaspoon baking
powder

1¼ cups whole milk

2 large eggs

Southern cornbread is traditionally baked in a cast-iron skillet, which creates a crispy crust. Baking cornbread in a baking dish makes it easier to take to gatherings; the flavor is just as good, though the texture is slightly softer.

MAKES 12 SLICES

Preheat the oven to 400°.

Melt 7 tablespoons of the butter and set aside. Use the remaining butter to grease a 9 × 11-inch baking dish.

Stir together the flour, cornmeal, sugar, salt, and baking powder. In a separate bowl, whisk together the melted butter, milk, and eggs.

Fold the wet ingredients into dry just until there are no lumps. Pour into a greased baking dish and bake for 25–30 minutes, until golden and a toothpick comes out clean when inserted into the center.

Double Jalapeño Havarti Cornbread

This cornbread recipe is special for three reasons. First, I combine fresh and pickled jalapeños for a tart green, spicy flavor. Second, the Havarti adds creaminess that complements the sharp pepper. Third, adding onion powder to the mix amps up the savory flavor. As soon as I pulled this from the oven it became my favorite cornbread recipe.

MAKES 12 SLICES

Preheat the oven to 400°.

Melt 7 tablespoons of the butter and set aside. Use the remaining butter to grease a 9 × 11-inch baking dish.

Stir together the flour, cornmeal, sugar, salt, baking powder, onion powder, fresh jalapeños, and Havarti cubes. In a separate bowl, whisk together the melted butter, milk, eggs, and pickled jalapeños.

Fold the wet ingredients into the dry just until there are no lumps. Pour into a greased baking dish and bake for 25–30 minutes, until golden and a toothpick inserted in the center comes out clean. Allow to cool for 15 minutes before slicing. Can be served warm or at room temperature.

8 tablespoons (1 stick) butter, divided

½ cup plus 2 tablespoons all-purpose flour

1¾ cups yellow or white cornmeal

1 tablespoon plus 1 teaspoon granulated sugar

1¼ teaspoons kosher or sea salt

1 tablespoon plus 1 teaspoon baking powder

2 teaspoons onion powder (not onion salt)

1 large, fresh jalapeño pepper, stem, white membrane, and seeds removed, green flesh, minced

4 ounces Havarti cheese, cubed (about 1 cup)

½ cup pickled jalapeño slices, drained and minced

1¼ cups whole milk

2 large eggs

(V) = vegan

A

All-Purpose Pie Dough, 92
appetizers
    Boiled Peanuts (V), 14
    Crunchy Buttermilk Fried Pickle
        Chips, 21
    Deviled Eggs with Pickled Okra,
        27
    Easy-Peasy Cheese Straws, 22
    Edisto Island Crispy, Curried
        Deviled Eggs, 28
    Garden Stuffed Summer
        Tomatoes (V), 24
    Kale Chips (V), 30
    Kentucky Beer Cheese, 17–18
    Okra Chips (V), 26
    Pimento Cheese Deviled Eggs, 29
    Sassy Pimento Cheese, 25
    Slow-Cooker Boiled Peanuts (V),
        15
    Southern "Sausage" and Cheese
        Balls, 19
    Warm Corn Dip, 16
    Warm Sweet Onion Dip, 23
Apple Butter, Overnight, 148
Artichoke Relish, Easy, 158

B

Bacon, Fake-on, 131
Baked Limpin' Susan, 124
Baked Nashville Hot Cauliflower
    with Nashville Hot Sauce,
    65–67
BBQ Sauce (V), 76
Beans and Greens, 111
Beef Gravy for Rice (V), 60
black beans, 9
Boiled Peanuts (V), 14
Boiled Peanuts, Slow-Cooker (V), 15

bread
    Cheddar and Herb Biscuits, 164
    Cornbread, 170
    Double Jalapeño Havarti
        Cornbread, 171
    Easy Drop Biscuits, 168
    Hoecakes, 169
    Slow Cooker Pecan Cinnamon
        Rolls with Buttermilk–Cream
        Cheese Glaze, 166–67
Broccoli Bake, Three-Cheese, 86
Broccoli, Crisp, and Smoked
    Almond Salad, 116
broth
    Chickpea Broth (V), 35
    Corncob and Leek Broth (V), 32
    Roasted Vegetable Broth (V), 33
    Umami Mushroom Broth (V), 38
Brown Rice with Mushrooms (V),
    121
Brunswick Stew (V), 53

C

Carolina Grits with Sweet Potato
    Swirl and Smoked Gouda, 149
Carolina Veggie Burger, 83
cauliflower, 9
Cauliflower, Roasted, Étouffée (V),
    50
Cauliflower "Rice" with Fresh Herbs
    (V), 122
Charleston's Country Captain (V), 71
chayote squash, 10
Cheddar and Herb Biscuits, 164
Cheddar Corn Pudding, 88
cheese
    Cheese Grits Casserole, 90
    Cheesy Garlic Stuffed Potatoes,
        107

Easy-Peasy Cheese Straws, 22
Kentucky Beer Cheese, 17–18
Sassy Pimento Cheese, 25
Southern "Sausage" and Cheese
  Balls, 19
Chicken and Dumplings (V), 49
Chickpea Broth (V), 35
Chili, Slow-Cooker Green Tomato
  (V), 52
Chocolate Gravy, 61
Chow-Chow (V), 127
Coleslaw, Sweet and Tangy, 135
Company Succotash, 113
corn
  Corn Bisque, 39
  Corncob and Leek Broth (V), 32
  Corn Pudding, Cheddar, 88
  Warm Corn Dip, 16
  Winter Creamed Corn, 117
Cornbread, 170
Cornbread, Double Jalapeño
  Havarti, 171
Cornbread, Sage, and "Sausage"
  Dressing, 128
Crab Cakes, 77–79
Creamy Stovetop Mac and Cheese,
  106
Crisp Broccoli and Smoked Almond
  Salad, 115
Crunchy Buttermilk Fried Pickle
  Chips, 21
Crunchy Tomato Pie, 102–4

D
Deviled Eggs, Pimento Cheese, 29
Deviled Eggs with Pickled Okra, 27
Dill Pickled Beets (V), 156
Dirty Rice, 119
Double Jalapeño Havarti Cornbread,
  171
Dressing, Cornbread, Sage, and
  "Sausage," 128

E
Easy Artichoke Relish (V), 158
Easy Drop Biscuits, 168
Easy-Peasy Cheese Straws, 22
Edisto Island Crispy, Curried
  Deviled Eggs, 28
eggplant, 10
eggs
  Deviled Eggs with Pickled Okra,
    27
  Edisto Island Crispy, Curried
    Deviled Eggs, 28
  Pimento Cheese Deviled Eggs, 29

F
Fake-on Bacon (V), 131
Fried Green Tomatoes, 150
Fried Okra, 133

G
Garden Stuffed Summer Tomatoes
  (V), 24
Garlic powder, 11
Georgia Peanut Soup, 41
gravies
  Beef Gravy for Rice (V), 60
  Chocolate Gravy, 61
  Herb Gravy (V), 59
  Sawmill Gravy, 56
  Tomato Gravy, 55
grits
  Carolina Grits with Sweet Potato
    Swirl and Smoked Gouda, 149
  Cheese Grits Casserole, 90
  Sweet Breakfast Grits, 146
  Truffle and Mushroom Grits,
    144–45
Gumbo (V), 47

H
Herb Gravy (V), 59
Hoecakes, 169

Hoppin' John, 123
Hushpuppies, 143

I

Individual Crunchy Mac and
    Cheese, 118

J

jackfruit, 9
Jambalaya, 44

K

Kale Chips (V), 30
Kentucky Beer Cheese, 17–18

L

lentils, 9
liquid smoke, 11

M

Mac and Cheese, Creamy Stovetop,
    106
Mac and Cheese, Individual
    Crunchy, 118
Mac and Cheese, One-Pot Pimento,
    130
main dishes
    Baked Nashville Hot Cauliflower
        with Nashville Hot Sauce,
        65–67
    Carolina Veggie Burger, 83
    Charleston's Country Captain
        (V), 71
    Cheddar Corn Pudding, 88
    Cheese Grits Casserole, 90
    Crab Cakes, 77–79
    Oyster Po' Boys, 81
    Pulled "Pork" Barbecue (V), 74
    Slow-Cooker BBQ Cabbage Rolls,
        84–85
    Southern Fried Tofu Nuggets,
        68–70

Three-Cheese Broccoli Bake, 86
    Tomato Pudding, 89
    Vegetable Purloo (V), 72
Memphis Mustard Slaw, 138
miso paste, 10
Mississippi Comeback Sauce, 134
mushrooms, 9
    Umami Mushroom Broth (V), 38

O

Okra Chips (V), 26
Old-School Buttermilk Mashed
    Potatoes, 114
One-Pot Pimento Mac and Cheese,
    130
onions
    onion juice, 12
    onion powder, 11
    Tickled Pink Onions (V), 161
    Warm Sweet Onion Dip, 23
Overnight Apple Butter (V), 148
Oyster Po' Boys, 81

P

Parmigiano-Reggiano cheese and
    rinds, 10
peanuts
    Boiled Peanuts (V), 14
    Georgia Peanut Soup, 41
    Slow-Cooker Boiled Peanuts (V),
        15
pickles
    Crunchy Buttermilk Fried Pickle
        Chips, 21
    Dill Pickled Beets (V), 156
    Easy Artichoke Relish (V), 158
    Pickled Okra (V), 155
    Salted Carrot Coins (V), 162
    Tickled Pink Onions (V), 161
Pie Dough, All-Purpose, 92
pies, savory
    All-Purpose Pie Dough, 92

Crunchy Tomato Pie, 102–4
Ribbon Pie, 93–95
Roasted Vegetable Potpie with
    Cream Cheese Peppercorn
    Crust, 100–101
Vegetable Stuffed Pie, 97–98
Vidalia Onion and Clemson Blue
    Pie with Pecan Pretzel Crust,
    99
Pimento Aioli, 151
Pimento Cheese Deviled Eggs, 29
Potlikker Greens (V), 142
Pulled "Pork" Barbecue (V), 74

R
rice
    Brown Rice with Mushrooms, 121
    Savannah Red Rice (V), 120
Roasted Butter Beans with Garlic
    (V), 125
Roasted Cauliflower Étouffée (V),
    50
Roasted Vegetable Broth (V), 33
Roasted Vegetable Potpie with
    Cream Cheese Peppercorn
    Crust, 100–101
Rutmus, 139
Ribbon Pie, 93–95

S
Salted Caramel Bourbon Pecan
    Sweet Potato Soufflé, 109–10
Salted Carrot Coins (V), 162
Sassy Pimento Cheese, 25
sauces
    BBQ Sauce (V), 76
    Mississippi Comeback Sauce, 134
    Nashville Hot Sauce, 67
Savannah Red Rice (V), 120
Sawmill Gravy, 56
seitan (processed wheat gluten), 7
Senate Bean Soup (V), 36–37

Slow-Cooker BBQ Cabbage Rolls,
    84–85
Slow-Cooker Black-Eyed Peas (V),
    126
Slow-Cooker Boiled Peanuts (V), 15
Slow-Cooker Green Tomato Chili
    (V), 52
Slow-Cooker Pecan Cinnamon
    Rolls with Buttermilk–Cream
    Cheese Glaze, 166–67
smoked paprika, 11
smoked salts and peppers, 11
soups
    Corn Bisque, 39
    Georgia Peanut Soup, 41
    Senate Bean Soup (V), 36–37
    Tomato Essence Soup (V), 43
    Winter Tomato and Rice Soup
        (V), 42
Southern Fried Tofu Nuggets,
    68–70
Southern "Sausage" and Cheese
    Balls, 19
soy sauce, 11
Spicy Tomato Aspic (V), 141
stews
    Brunswick Stew (V), 53
    Chicken and Dumplings (V), 49
    Gumbo (V), 47
    Jambalaya, 44
    Roasted Cauliflower Étouffée (V),
        50
    Slow-Cooker Green Tomato Chili
        (V), 52
Stuffed Yellow Summer Squash, 152
Sweet and Tangy Coleslaw (V), 135
Sweet Breakfast Grits, 146

T
tempeh (fermented soybeans), 8
texturized vegetable protein, 8
Three-Cheese Broccoli Bake, 86

Tickled Pink Onions (V), 161
tofu (soybeans), 6
tomatoes
    Crunchy Tomato Pie, 102–4
    Fried Green Tomatoes, 150
    Garden Stuffed Summer
        Tomatoes (V), 24
    Spicy Tomato Aspic (V), 141
    Tomato Essence Soup (V), 43
    Tomato Gravy, 55
    tomato paste, 11
    Tomato Pudding, 89
    Winter Tomato and Rice Soup
        (V), 42
Truffle and Mushroom Grits,
    144–45
Twice-Baked Not-So-Sweet
    Potatoes, 136–37

U
Umami Mushroom Broth (V), 38

V
vegan recipes
    Baked Limpin' Susan (V), 124
    BBQ Sauce, 76
    Beans and Greens, 111
    Beef Gravy for Rice, 60
    Boiled Peanuts, 14
    Brown Rice with Mushrooms,
        121
    Brunswick Stew, 53
    Cauliflower "Rice" with Fresh
        Herbs, 122
    Charleston's Country Captain, 71
    Chicken and Dumplings, 49
    Chickpea Broth, 35
    Chow-Chow, 127
    Corncob and Leek Broth, 32
    Dill Pickled Beets, 156
    Easy Artichoke Relish, 158
    Fake-on Bacon, 131

Garden Stuffed Summer
    Tomatoes, 24
Gumbo, 47
Herb Gravy, 59
Kale Chips, 30
Memphis Mustard Slaw, 138
Okra Chips, 26
Overnight Apple Butter, 148
Pickled Okra, 155
Potlikker Greens, 142
Pulled "Pork" Barbecue, 74
Roasted Butter Beans with Garlic,
    125
Roasted Cauliflower Étouffée, 50
Roasted Vegetable Broth, 33
Salted Carrot Coins, 162
Savannah Red Rice, 120
Senate Bean Soup, 36–37
Slow-Cooker Black-Eyed Peas,
    126
Slow-Cooker Boiled Peanuts, 15
Slow-Cooker Green Tomato
    Chili, 52
Spicy Tomato Aspic, 141
Sweet and Tangy Coleslaw, 135
Tickled Pink Onions, 161
Tomato Essence Soup, 43
Umami Mushroom Broth, 38
Vegetable Purloo, 72
Winter Tomato and Rice Soup, 42
Vegetable Purloo, 72
vegetables and side dishes
    Baked Limpin' Susan (V), 124
    Beans and Greens (V), 111
    Brown Rice with Mushrooms (V),
        121
    Carolina Grits with Sweet Potato
        Swirl and Smoked Gouda, 149
    Cauliflower "Rice" with Fresh
        Herbs (V), 122
    Cheesy Garlic Stuffed Potatoes,
        107

Chow-Chow (V), 127

Company Succotash, 113

Cornbread, Sage, and "Sausage" Dressing, 128

Creamy Stovetop Mac and Cheese, 106

Crisp Broccoli and Smoked Almond Salad, 115

Dirty Rice, 119

Fake-on Bacon (V), 131

Fried Green Tomatoes, 150

Fried Okra, 133

Hoppin' John, 123

Hushpuppies, 143

Individual Crunchy Mac and Cheese, 118

Memphis Mustard Slaw (V), 138

Mississippi Comeback Sauce, 134

Old-School Buttermilk Mashed Potatoes, 114

One-Pot Pimento Mac and Cheese, 130

Overnight Apple Butter (V), 148

Pimento Aioli, 151

Potlikker Greens (V), 142

Roasted Butter Beans with Garlic (V), 125

Rutmus, 139

Salted Caramel Bourbon Pecan Sweet Potato Soufflé, 109–10

Savannah Red Rice (V), 120

Slow-Cooker Black-Eyed Peas (V), 126

Spicy Tomato Aspic (V), 141

Stuffed Yellow Summer Squash, 152

Sweet and Tangy Coleslaw (V), 135

Sweet Breakfast Grits, 146

Truffle and Mushroom Grits, 144–45

Twice-Baked Not-So-Sweet Potatoes, 136–37

Wilmer's Potato Salad, 140

Winter Creamed Corn, 117

Vegetable Stuffed Pie, 97–98

Veggie Burger, Carolina, 83

Vidalia Onion and Clemson Blue Pie with Pecan Pretzel Crust, 99

W

Warm Corn Dip, 16

Warm Sweet Onion Dip, 23

Wilmer's Potato Salad, 140

Winter Creamed Corn, 117

Winter Tomato and Rice Soup (V), 42